HARRISON COUNTY PRIMARY SCHOOL
HARRISON ROAD
FAREHAM
HAMPSHI...
CW01619019

Teaching about World Faiths:

curriculum support for teachers

BUDDHISM

CHRISTIANITY

HINDUISM

ISLAM

JUDAISM

SIKHISM

Essex County Council
Education

CONTENTS

HARRISON COUNTY PRIMARY SCHOOL
HARRISON ROAD
FAREHAM
HAMPSHIRE PO16 7EQ

page i **Introduction**

1 **Buddhism**

15 **Christianity**

31 **Hinduism**

55 **Islam**

71 **Judaism**

91 **Sikhism**

ACKNOWLEDGEMENTS

Authors: Heather Dovey-Laytham
Robert Dovey-Laytham
Lynn Gent
Andrew Scott
Anne Stafford

The material has been checked for accuracy by members of the appropriate faith communities.

Illustrations and Design: Tania Field

The Essex Standing Advisory Council for Religious Education has supported the production of this document and approved the final version.

FURTHER READING

Brown A. et al, **Religions**, Longman, 1988
Cole W. O., **Six Religions in the Twentieth Century**, Hulton, 1984
Erricker C. (ed), **Teaching World Religions**, Heinemann, 1993
Smart N., **The World's Religions**, Cambridge University Press, 1989
The World's Religions, Lion, 1982
Brown A. (ed), **Festivals in World Religions**, Longman, 1986
Gateshill P. and Thompson J., **Religious Artefacts in the Classroom**, Hodder and Stoughton, 1992

Published by Essex Development and Advisory Service,
Education Department.

ISBN 0 9044 2825 7

© Essex County Council Education, 1995

Further copies may be obtained from:
EDAS Publications
Wickford Centre
Alderney Gardens
Wickford
Essex SS11 7JZ

Price: £15

Religions of the world

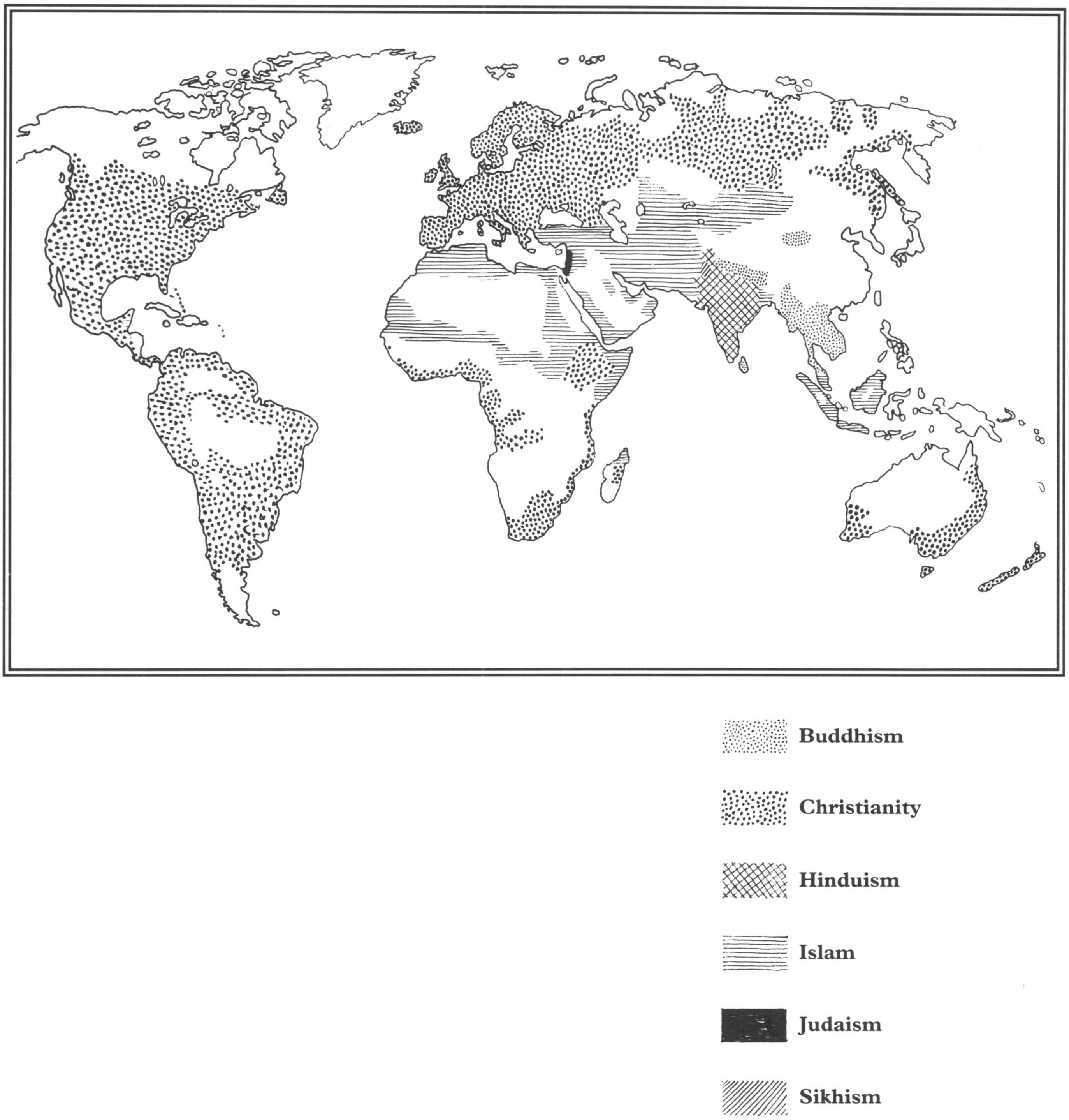

RITES OF PASSAGE	PLACES OF WORSHIP	RITUAL OBJECTS AND ARTEFACTS	SYMBOLS
Page 9 Initiation Death	**Page 10** The Vihara Relic mounds The Bodhi tree	**Pages 11 to 13** Images of the Buddha Images of the Bodhisattvas The Wheel of Life Mandalas Thankas Prayer wheels Prayer beads Dorje and bell	**Page 13** The eight spoked wheel The lotus
Pages 22 to 23 Birth Coming of age Marriage Death	**Pages 24 to 27** Church of England churches Roman Catholic churches Orthodox churches Baptist chapels Religious Society of Friends' (Quakers) meeting houses Salvation Army halls or citadels The Eucharist Sacraments The Lord's Prayer Priests, Bishops etc.	**Pages 27 to 30** Crosses Devotional statues Icons Paten and chalice Incense Baptism Advent Holy Week Liturgical colours	**Page 30** The cross The Chi Ro The IHS The Alpha and Omega The fish The dove
Pages 43 to 45 Birth Coming of age Marriage Death	**Pages 45 to 47** The Mandir Congregational Puja Centres of pilgrimage	**Pages 47 to 52** Images of deities Puja tray Divas Rakhis Mala beads Mendhi patterns Garlands Bindi Mandalas/Yantras	**Pages 52 to 53** Aum Swastika
Pages 65 to 66 Birth Coming of age Marriage Death	**Page 67** The Masjid	**Page 68** Qur'an and stand Prayer	**Page 69** Crescent moon and star
Pages 83 to 84 Birth Coming of age Marriage Death	**Pages 84 to 85** The Synagogue The Western Wall	**Pages 86 to 88** Scrolls Clothing Shabbat Rosh Hashanah Hanukkah Purim The Seder service	**Page 89** Magen David Menorah
Pages 97 to 99 Birth Coming of age Marriage Death	**Pages 99 to 100** The Gurdwara Worship at the Gurdwara The Harmandir at Amritsar	**Pages 100 to 104** Clothing Images of the Gurus and the Harmandir Khanda and steel bowl Guru Granth Sahib Prayer	Khanda

INTRODUCTION

The Education Reform Act 1988 requires that:
'Any Agreed Syllabus... shall reflect the fact that the religious traditions in Great Britain are in the main Christian whilst taking account of the teaching and practices of the other principal religions represented in Great Britain'.

All Local Education Authorities (LEAs) are required by the Education Act 1993 to review their Agreed Syllabuses in the light of this requirement, which means that schools will now have to enure that pupils learn about many different religions.

This document has been produced in order to help teachers to meet this requirement. It is not intended for use with pupils, nor does it provide suggestions of teaching and learning strategies. Many excellent publications containing practical ideas for RE are available elsewhere.

A major obstacle to meeting the demands of the law is that many non-specialist teachers do not feel confident in their own understanding of different world religions. This document seeks to provide teachers, particularly non-specialists, with an overview of Buddhism, Christianity, Hinduism, Islam, Judaism and Sikhism. Many LEAs have interpreted these six religions as being the 'principal religions represented in Great Britain', and the School Curriculum and Assessment Authority (SCAA) features these religions in the two Model Agreed Syllabuses which it has published.

One of the main difficulties that the writers faced was with regard to the degree of detail that the material should contain. Many published 'summaries' of world religions do not do justice to their complexity and to the variety of beliefs and practices that exist within different traditions. A degree of over-simplification and superficiality is inevitable when trying to condense such a vast range of information into a few pages, but we have striven to achieve accuracy at all times and we hope that nothing contained within the document will cause offense to adherents of the religions that have been covered.

Members of the appropriate faith communities have read through the material and have made many helpful suggestions which have been incorporated into the text. We are grateful to them for taking the time to assist us in this way.

The spellings, transliterations and definitions of religious terms are consistent with those contained in the '*Glossary of Terms*' which accompanied the SCAA Model Agreed Syllabuses.
(A copy of the Glossary was sent to every school by SCAA – further copies are available from SCAA).
Literal translations into English are printed in (*italics*).

Dates are designated CE (Common Era, equivalent to AD) and BCE (Before the Common Era, equivalent to BC).

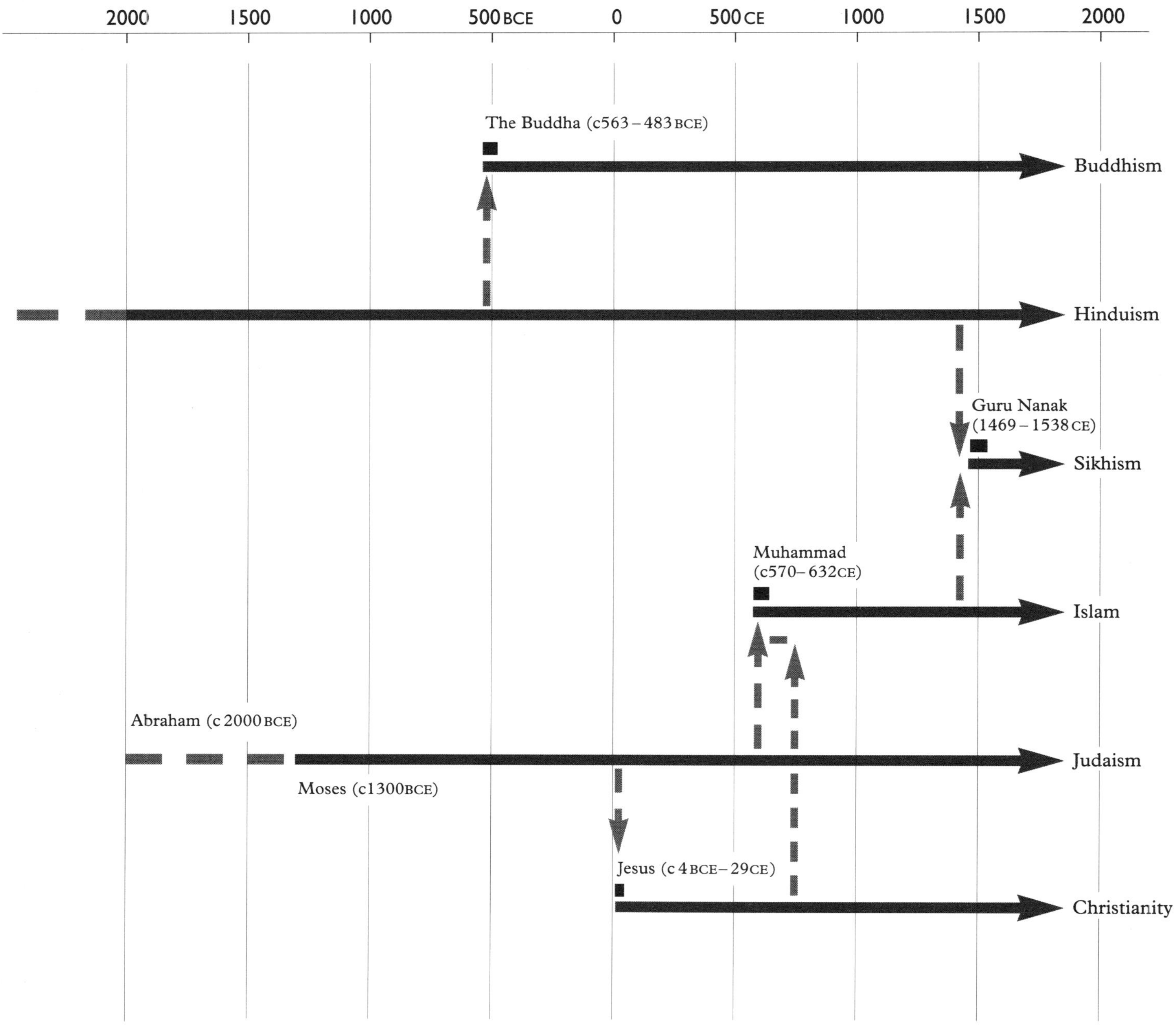
2000
1500
1000
500 BCE
0
500 CE
1000
1500
2000
The Buddha (c563 – 483 BCE)
Buddhism
Hinduism
Guru Nanak
(1469 – 1538 CE)
Sikhism
Muhammad
(c570– 632CE)
Islam
Abraham (c 2000 BCE)
Judaism
Moses (c1300BCE)
Jesus (c 4 BCE– 29CE)
Christianity

	BACKGROUND INFORMATION	BELIEFS AND WAY OF LIFE	WRITINGS	FESTIVALS
Buddhism	**Pages 1 to 3** Origins The Buddha Mahayana and Theravada Buddhism Variety within Buddhism Buddhists today	**Pages 3 to 6** The Three Signs of Being The Tiratana or Trisharana The Four Noble Truths The Noble Eightfold Path The Precepts The Brahma Viharas Meditation Kamma, Samsara. the Khandas and Nibbana Bodhisattvas	**Page 7** The Suttas The Pali Canon Jataka tales	**Pages 7 to 8** Wesak Asala Perahara The Kathina Ceremony
Christianity	**Pages 15 to 16** Origins Jesus Paul The Church Christians today	**Pages 17 to 18** The Nicene Creed The Trinity The Incarnation The Resurrection Values	**Pages 18 to 19** The Bible The New Testament	**Pages 19 to 21** Advent Christmas Epiphany Candlemas Shrove Tuesday Ash Wednesday Lent Holy Week Palm Sunday Maundy Thursday Good Friday Holy Saturday Easter Day Ascension Day Whitsun
Hinduism	**Page 31** Origins India Hindus today	**Pages 31 to 36** Brahman and Atman One and many The Avatars of Vishnu Shiva and Parvati Nature gods and animal gods Reincarnation Samsara and Karma Four paths to liberation Varnas Ashramas Dharma Ahimsa Puja in the home	**Pages 37 to 39** Shruti and Smriti The Four Vedas The Upanishads The Mahabharata The Ramayana The Laws of Manu The Puranas The Panchatantra and the Hitopadesh	**Pages 39 to 43** Divali Vasanta Panchami/ Saraswati Puja Holi Ramnavami Ratha-Yatra/Jagannatha Raksha Bandhan Janmashtami Ganesha-Chaturthi Navaratri/Durga Puja/ Dassehra/ Vijay Dashami
Islam	**Pages 55 to 57** Origins Muhammad Sunnis and Shi'ahs Sufis Muslims today	**Pages 57 to 60** Allah Angels Shari'ah Law The Five Pillars Visual art	**Pages 61 to 63** The Qur'an The Hadith and the Sirah Sufi literature	**Pages 63 to 64** Id-ul-Fitr Il-ul-Adha
Judaism	**Pages 71 to 72** Origins The Patriarchs Jewish history Jews today	**Pages 73 to 74** God The Messiah and the Kingdom of God Torah and Mitzvot Kashrut The home Shabbat	**Pages 75 to 76** The Tenakh The Torah Nevi'im Ketuvim The Talmud	**Pages 76 to 82** Rosh Hashanah Yom Kippur Sukkot Simchat Torah Hanukkah Tu bi-Shvat Purim Pesach Yom ha-Shoah Yom ha-Atzmaut Shavuot Tishah b'Av
Sikhism	**Pages 91 to 93** Origins The ten Gurus Guru Nanak Guru Gobind Singh Sikhs today	**Page 94** Basic beliefs God The purpose of life Diet	**Page 95** The Guru Granth Sahib The Dasam Granth	**Pages 96 to 97** Baisakhi Divali Hola Mohalla Gurpurbs

Buddhism

The man who is disturbed by wrong thoughts,
whose selfish passions are strong
and who only seeks sensuous pleasures
increases his craving desires and makes stronger
the chains he forges for himself.

But he who enjoys peaceful thoughts,
who considers the sorrows of pleasure,
and who ever remembers the light of his life –
he will see the end of his cravings,
he will break the chains of death.

The Dhammapada 349 – 350

Buddhism

BACKGROUND INFORMATION

THE BUDDHA

Siddattha Gotama (c.563-483BCE) was born in present-day Nepal. His father, Suddhodana, was the leader of a tribal group called the Sakyas (another name for the Buddha is Sakyamuni, meaning 'Sage of the Sakyas'). Before Siddattha's birth, his mother dreamed that a white elephant entered her side. This indicated that her child would grow up to become a great person. She gave birth resting against a tree in a garden called Lumbini. The story goes that the baby emerged painlessly from her side, and was immediately able to walk and talk.

A soothsayer at Suddhodana's court informed him that his son would grow up to be either a great world ruler or a holy man. Suddhodana knew that to live as a holy man was to live a life of asceticism and privation. This, coupled with the fact that his wife had died within a week of Siddattha's birth, made Suddhodana determined to shield his son from all forms of suffering. As a result, Siddattha grew up in great luxury. He lived in a magnificent palace and was completely protected from the harsh realities of life. Eventually he married and had a son, but he was dissatisfied with his existence.

Curious about life outside the confines of his palace, Siddattha gained his father's permission to visit a nearby town. He visited the town four times, and on each occasion he was confronted by the fact that suffering is an inescapable part of the human condition. On his first three visits he saw an old man, a sick man and a dead body. On his fourth visit he saw a Sadhu, a holy man who had given up all worldly pleasures and possessions.

Siddattha decided that he too would give up everything and search for the answer to the question: 'Why do people suffer?' He left his family in the care of relatives, gave away his clothes and jewellery and set out to find the answer he craved. It is said that he was 29 years old.

After spending time with some spiritual teachers, from whom he learned the techniques of meditation, Siddattha joined a group of five Sadhus. He spent several years in their company, subjecting himself to extremes of self-denial, and going without food, shelter and any sort of comfort. His body became so emaciated and weak that he became ill and eventually he collapsed from exhaustion. Now Siddattha decided to leave his five companions and to take food and rest. When his strength returned, he decided to follow the Middle Way, treading between the two extremes of self-indulgence and self-mortification.

ORIGINS

Buddhism started not with a revelation from God (Buddhists do not believe in a personal God), but with the quest of a man who wanted to find out how to end suffering. The man was Siddattha Gotama, later known as the Buddha, who lived in Northern India nearly 2,500 years ago.

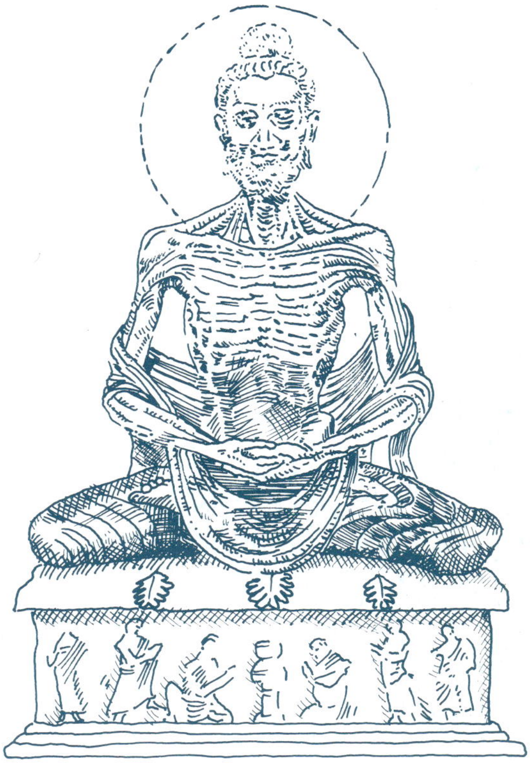

Above: *An image of Siddattha Gotama after many years of extreme deprivation, almost starving to death.*

Left: *Buddha at the moment of enlightenment, surrounded with scenes illustrating events from his life. Burma, 12th to 13th century.*

Note: As Buddhism spread, it came to be expressed in many different languages, including Pali, Sanskrit, Japanese and Tibetan. Pali versions of Buddhist terms are generally used in this text.

One night, under a full moon, Siddattha sat in a forest glade under a tree and began to meditate. Mara, the Buddhist personification of evil and death, sent many temptations in order to distract him, but Siddattha's resolve remained firm. He successfully resisted all temptations, and he at last reached a state of perfect peace and awareness. He had attained Nibbana, the 'blowing out' of the fires of greed, hatred and delusion, and he had become the Buddha (*the Enlightened* or *Awakened One*). The glade later became known as Bodh Gaya (*the Place of Enlightenment* or *Awakening*) and the tree under which he sat became known as the Bodhi tree (*the Tree of Enlightenment* or *Awakening*).

The Buddha was 35 years old when he achieved enlightenment, and he devoted the rest of his life to travelling throughout India, spreading the wisdom that he had acquired. His first sermon was given in the Deer Park at Varanasi or Banaras. His audience consisted of the five Sadhus with whom he had travelled before his enlightenment. When he had left them, they had mocked him for his lack of perseverance, but now they recognised the truth of his teaching and they became his first followers.

As the number of his disciples grew, the Sangha (the *community* of monks and nuns) was formed. He revisited his wife and son, and they joined the Sangha. When he was 80, he became ill after eating some food. He died and entered into his Parinibbana, his final and complete Nibbana (see page 6).

MAHAYANA AND THERAVADA BUDDHISM

From India, Buddhism spread to the north and east (to countries such as Tibet, China, Korea and Japan) and to the south and east (to countries such as Sri Lanka, Thailand, Cambodia, Laos, Burma and Vietnam). Ironically, in India itself Buddhism all but died out until its reintroduction in 1956.

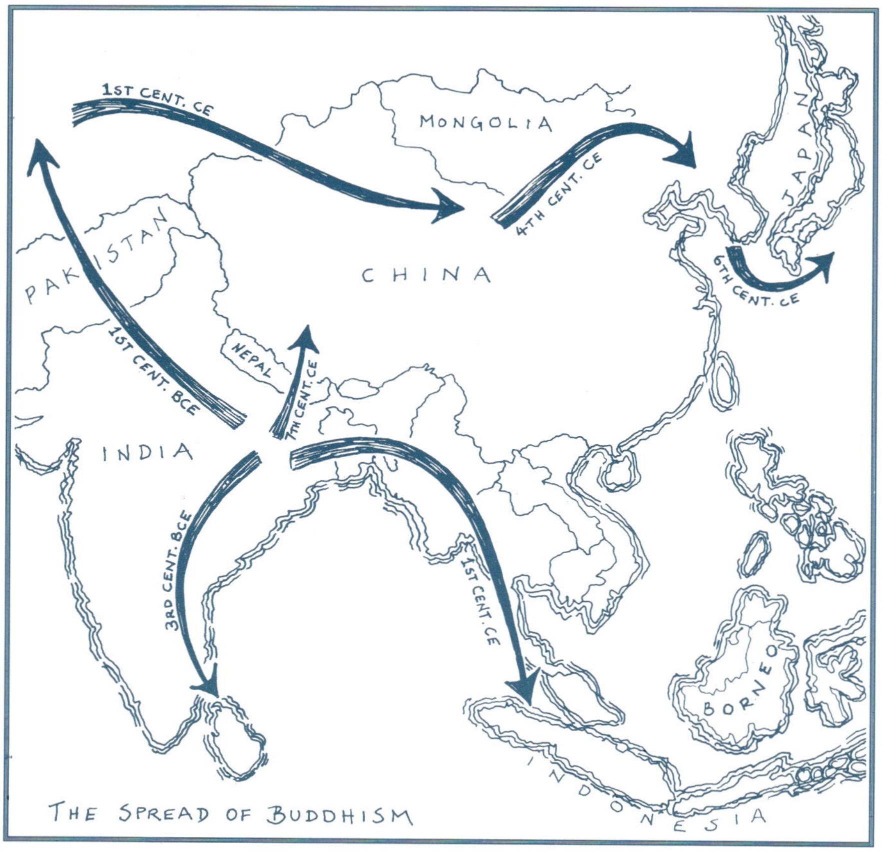

The school of Buddhism associated with countries lying to the north and east of India is known as Mahayana (*Great Way* or *Vehicle*). It includes Tibetan Buddhism, Zen Buddhism and Pure Land Buddhism.

The school of Buddhism associated with countries lying to the south and east of India is known as Theravada (*Way of the Elders*). A form of Buddhism known as Vajrayana or Tantric Buddhism, which came to fruition in Tibet, is associated with the Mahayana school, but it is often regarded as a third tradition within Buddhism.

Pali is the language of the texts of the Theravada school. Most of the Buddhist terms used in this text are given in their Pali versions. Sanskrit is generally used in the Mahayana tradition. Zen Buddhism uses terms expressed in Japanese, and Tibetan Buddhism uses terms expressed in Tibetan.

VARIETY WITHIN BUDDHISM

'Buddhism' is a Western term. Adherents to this religion prefer to refer to it as the Dhamma (*Universal Law* or *Ultimate Truth*) or Buddha-dhamma. Buddhism is an umbrella term which covers a wide variety of beliefs, practices and cultural traditions.

Buddhism has a very tolerant view of other religions. As one of the Buddhist King Asoka's rock edicts proclaims: '*One should honour the religions of others, for in so doing one helps one's own religion to grow and renders service to the religions of others*' (3rd century BCE).

As Buddhism spread to different countries, it adapted and changed, absorbing many ideas and customs derived from local religious traditions. This helps to account for its tremendous richness and diversity, about which Guy Claxton has written: '*Buddhism in Sri Lanka, Buddhism in Tibet and Buddhism in Japan are as different on the surface as Christianity, Judaism and Islam*' (quoted in 'Buddhism' by Denise Cush).

BUDDHISTS TODAY

There are over 300 million Buddhists in the world today and around 130,000 in Britain. Throughout Britain, a wide variety of Buddhist groups and organisations are represented. Buddhism is often quoted as being the fastest-growing religion in the Western world.

BELIEFS AND WAY OF LIFE

THE THREE SIGNS OF BEING

The Three Signs of Being (Annica, Anatta and Dukkha) are perceived by Buddhists as underlying human existence.

Annica (*impermanence* or *transience*) is the state of constant change and instability that characterises everything that exists. Ultimately everyone and everything dies and ceases to exist.

Anatta (*no self* or *no soul*) is consistent with Annica. It is the idea that there is no permanent unchanging self or soul in anyone or anything.

Dukkha (*suffering, ill, unsatisfactoriness* or *imperfection*) is the idea that suffering and unsatisfactoriness are an unavoidable part of the human condition. Dukkha is the first Noble Truth (see page 4).

THE TIRATANA OR THE TRISHARANA

The Buddha, the Dhamma and the Sangha are referred to as the Tiratana (*the Triple Refuge*) or the Trisharana (*the Three Jewels*).

The ***Buddha*** is revered not as a god, but as a man who achieved enlightenment himself and then indicated the way by which others could achieve it for themselves.

The ***Dhamma*** (*Universal Law* or *Ultimate Truth*) is the teaching of the Buddha, summarised by the Four Noble Truths and the Noble Eightfold Path (see page 4).

Top: *Buddha preaching, seated upon a lotus, hands held in a symbolic gesture of teaching, 'turning of the wheel of the law' (see page 13). Western Pakistan, 2nd to 3rd century.*
Centre: *Vairocana Buddha (of Vajrayana Buddhism) depicted holding his hands in a position symbolising supreme wisdom. South Eastern Korea, 7th to 8th century.*
Bottom: *Teaching Buddha seated inside an aureole. Java, 8th century.*

Within Theravada Buddhism, the term ***Sangha*** tends to be restricted to the monastic community of Bhikkhus and Bhikkhunis (Buddhist monks and nuns). More usually, the term refers to the worldwide community comprising all who try to live according to the teachings of the Buddha.

THE FOUR NOBLE TRUTHS

1 ***Dukkha*** (*suffering, ill, unsatisfactoriness* or *imperfection*): all life contains suffering and everything is ultimately unsatisfactory.

2 ***Samudaya*** (*arising* or *origin* of Dukkha): suffering and unsatisfactoriness arise from Tanha (*thirst, craving* or *desire*).

3 ***Nirodha*** (*cessation* of Dukkha): the way to eliminate suffering and unsatisfactoriness is by learning to live without craving or desire.

4 ***The Middle Way*** (the Noble Eightfold Path): the way to live without craving or desire is by following the Middle Way, neither living in too much comfort nor in too great austerity, and by following the Noble Eightfold Path.

Above: *The Wheel is a symbol of the Dhamma (the teaching of the Buddha or Buddhism). The eight spokes represent the Eightfold Path.*

THE NOBLE EIGHTFOLD PATH

1 ***Right View or Understanding***: seeing things as they really are, seeing things in terms of Annica, Dukkha and Anatta.

2 ***Right Thought or Aspiration***: directing compassionate, loving thoughts to all living things.

3 ***Right Speech***: saying things that are of benefit to others and avoiding lies and insults.

4 ***Right Action***: behaving in a way that does no harm and which benefits others.

5 ***Right Livelihood***: earning a living in a way that does no harm and which benefits others.

6 ***Right Effort***: striving in an active way to follow the Noble Eightfold Path and to avoid distractions.

7 ***Right Mindfulness***: being constantly aware of the needs of others and paying full attention to whatever one is doing.

8 ***Right Concentration***: focusing the mind totally on one thing. This is achieved through meditation.

Buddhists have a strong ecological concern and try to live in balance and harmony with nature. Most Buddhists are vegetarians.

THE PRECEPTS

The **5** Precepts are basic rules for living which apply to all Buddhists:

1 To refrain from harming any living thing.
2 To refrain from taking what is not given.
3 To refrain from sexual misconduct.
4 To refrain from lying and using abusive speech.
5 To refrain from alcohol and other intoxicants which cloud the mind.

Bhikkhus (monks) and Bhikkhunis (nuns) promise to adhere to **10** Precepts. The additional five are:

6 To refrain from eating other than at prescribed times.
7 To refrain from dancing, singing, music making and unseemly public displays.
8 To refrain from using anything that will beautify personal appearance, for example make-up, perfume and jewellery.
9 To refrain from sleeping in a high or large bed.
10 To refrain from accepting gold and silver.

THE BRAHMA VIHARAS

The Brahma Viharas are the four sublime states stressed by the Buddha:
Metta (*loving kindness*, a pure love which is neither grasping nor possessive).
Karuna (*compassion*).
Mudita (*sympathetic joy*, rejoicing in the good fortune of others).
Upekkha (*equanimity* or *evenness of mind*).

Cultivation of the Brahma Viharas is believed to lead to the freeing of the mind.

MEDITATION

Meditation is an important practice for all Buddhists. Many methods of meditation have been developed in Buddhism, and different traditions favour different techniques. Two of the main forms of meditation are Samatha and Vipassana.

Samatha meditation seeks to develop calmness and control of the mind. It is initially concerned with the development of mindfulness: the ability to be aware of oneself and of the state that one is in. This might be achieved by concentrating on one particular thing to the exclusion of all else, until the point is reached when awareness of that particular thing totally fills the consciousness of the meditator. Beginners often start by focussing their attention solely on their breathing, allowing all distracting thoughts and feelings to drift out of their consciousness.

Above: *A Buddhist monk meditating.*
Below: *A lotus flower.*

Vipassana meditation is a more intellectual form of meditation which seeks to develop insight into the nature of reality. It involves deep contemplation of the truths of Buddhism, and analysis of the meditator's physical and mental states and of the surrounding environment.

Buddhists often use aids to meditation. These include objects such as stones, flowers, Mandalas (see page 12), and images of the Buddha and of Bodhisattvas (see page 11).

Buddhists also meditate by repeatedly chanting sacred sounds and phrases called Mantras. The best known Mantra is *'Om mani padme hum'*. This is usually translated rather inadequately as: *'Hail to the jewel in the lotus'*. One attempt at a literal translation of this Mantra reads: *'Hail to the diamond jewel of Nibbana in the wisdom and compassion of the lotus of Samsara. Welcome!'*

All schools of Buddhism attach great value to the practice of meditation. One such school is Zen, which developed in China and Japan. Zen means 'meditation'. Zazen is the practice of sitting meditation frequently practised by Zen Buddhists.

Zen Buddhists also use paradoxical puzzles called Koans to trick people out of their normal forms of reasoning and perceptions of reality, so that they can see things as they truly are. A well-known Zen Koan asks: *'What is the sound of one hand clapping?'*

KAMMA, SAMSARA, THE KHANDAS AND NIBBANA

Like Hindus, Buddhists believe in ***Kamma*** (Karma or *action*). They believe that present actions affect future ones. The difference between the Buddhist and Hindu understanding of Kamma is that for Buddhists, Kamma is only affected by actions that are deliberate or intentional.

Samsara (*everyday life*) is the continual cycle of life, death and rebirth. The Buddhist understanding of Samsara is again different from that of Hindus. Buddhists do not believe that people possess souls which, after death, pass from one body into another. In the Buddhist view, a person is made up of five ***Khandas*** (components): Rupa (*form*), Vedana (*feeling*), Sanna (*perception*), Sankhara (*mental/karmic formation*), and Vinnana (*consciousness*). When a person dies, the five Khandas disintegrate to be re-constituted in another body. The Buddhist ideal is to rid oneself of all of the Khandas. This happens when Nibbana is attained.

Nibbana (*blowing out*) can be seen as the ultimate goal of Buddhism. It cannot be described, but it is reached when greed, hatred and delusion are extinguished. To attain Nibbana is to escape from the round of life, death and rebirth and to achieve a state of perfect peace.

Note: In this section Buddihist terms are given in Sanskrit versions rather than in Pali versions.

BODHISATTVAS

Mahayana Buddhists believe that in addition to Siddhartha Gotama, the Buddha, there are and will be many other Buddhas. They also believe that people can be helped in their efforts to attain Nirvana by Bodhisattvas (*Wisdom Beings*). A Bodhisattva is a being destined for enlightenment because of his or her total commitment to helping others to reach Buddhahood.

Bodhisattvas can also be taken to be different manifestations of aspects of the enlightened mind, or manifestations of aspects of reality, especially compassion, wisdom and energy.

Avalokiteshvara, the Bodhisattva of Infinite Compassion, is the most popular Bodhisattva. He is sometimes called Avalokita, and in Tibet he is known as Chenresig. The Dalai Lama (*Great Ocean*) is believed to be an incarnation of Chenresig.

Other well-known Bodhisattvas are Manjugosha or Manjushri, who is the Bodhisattva of infinite wisdom; Vajrapani, who is the Bodhisattva of spiritual power and energy; and Tara, who is female and who like Avalokiteshvara represents compassion. Tara shares some of the features of Avalokiteshvara because she is supposed to have been born from the tears that he shed in response to the world's sufferings.

Top: *Maitreya (the Buddha as Bodhisattva), Korea.*
Centre: *Vajrapani, Tibet.*
Bottom: *Manjushri, Tibet.*

WRITINGS

THE SUTTAS

A vast number of sacred scriptures are used in the many different schools of Buddhism, but within Mahayana Buddhism, the Suttas (*texts*) are especially revered. Mahayana tradition holds that the Suttas record the actual words of the Buddha.

Mahayana Buddhists show reverence to the Suttas as a means of cultivating respect for the Dhamma. It is usual for the Suttas to be kept wrapped in cloth, and they are never placed directly on the ground. As a mark of respect, some Buddhists raise the scriptures to their foreheads after reading them. Tibetan Buddhists keep the Suttas in a special place of honour on their shrines.

THE PALI CANON

Within the Theravada tradition, the writings comprising the Pali Canon are considered to have special authority and are treated with particular respect.

The three sections of the Pali Canon are known as the Tipitaka (*the Three Baskets*). They comprise:

The Vinaya Pitaka, which contains the rules for the Sangha (the *community* of monks and nuns), including teaching related to the Four Noble Truths (see page 4) and the Noble Eightfold Path (see page 4).

The Sutta Pitaka, which includes teaching about Anatta (the idea that there is no self–see page 3), the Buddha's life story, and a well-known collection of the Buddha's discourses, called the Dhammapada.

The Abhidhamma Pitaka, which contains a systematic philosophical and psychological treatment of the teachings given in the Vinaya and Sutta Pitakas.

Above: *Buddha surmounted by the sacred serpent-king Muchalinda who sheltered him from a storm in Bodh Gaya. Cambodia, 12th century.*
Below: *The traditional form of the Sri Lankan stupa at Anuradhapura.*
Bottom: *Worshipping deity, performing puja (devotion). Chinese Turkestan, 600 to 800CE.*

JATAKA TALES

Jataka literally means 'birth stories'. The Jataka collection contains moral stories which tell of the previous lives of the Buddha. Like Aesop's fables, the tales often feature animals as the central characters.

FESTIVALS

Festivals are an important feature of many Buddhist countries. The major festivals are celebrated on or near days which coincide with the full moon. Some Buddhist festivals are celebrated in many different countries, others are distinctive of particular countries. The customs associated with festivals vary from country to country, and the time of year that the festivals takes place also varies. Some festivals that take place in Buddhist countries are not really religious festivals at all. New Year, which is an important celebration in many Buddhist countries, has little to do with Buddhism. Some of the main festivals that are practised in Theravada countries, such as Sri Lanka, Thailand and Burma, are described in the text that follows.

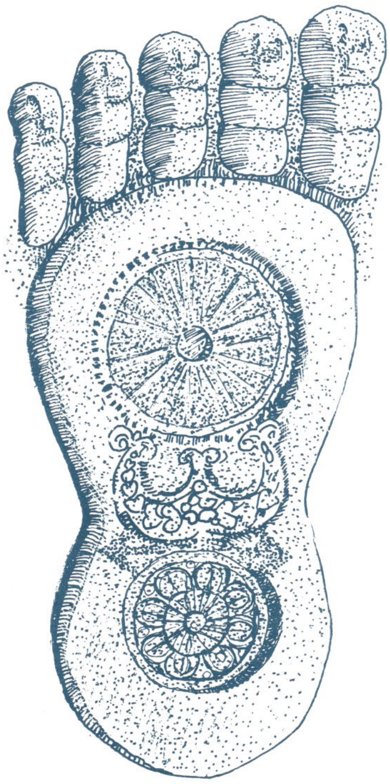

WESAK (May/June)

The Indian name for the second month is Vaisakha, and the Sinhalese name derived from it is Wesak. The term Wesak therefore denotes both the festival and the month in which it occurs. Wesak is the most important of Theravada festivals, commemorating the birth, enlightenment and death of the Buddha. In many countries, such as Sri Lanka and Thailand, an important feature of the festival is the lighting of lamps after dark, symbolising the enlightenment of the Buddha.

Customs associated with the festival vary from country to country, but the following features are typical. Wesak cards are sent to family and friends. Houses are cleaned and decorated. Offerings of flowers are made in temples, at shrines and at places associated with the Buddha. Captive birds are released. Children are told Jataka tales (see page 7).

ASALA PERAHARA (July/August)

Asala Perahara (*Procession of the Month of Asala*) is the most spectacular of all Sri Lankan celebrations. The festival takes place in Kandy, where there is a temple which houses the Buddha's tooth relic. After 15 days of colourful processions, a replica of the tooth relic is carried on the back of an elephant through the crowded streets, accompanied by flag-bearers, musicians, dancers and many other elephants. The actual tooth relic is too precious to leave the temple in which it is kept.

THE KATHINA CEREMONY (November)

In Sri Lanka, the month of Asala marks the beginning of Vas, the Rains Retreat. The Rains Retreat is an important feature of the monastic calendar in Theravada countries. The timing of the Rains Retreat varies according to the rainy season in different countries, but it always lasts for three months. It is a time when Bhikkhus (monks) and Bhikkhunis (nuns) devote themselves to study and meditation. Lay Buddhists can join them for all or part of the Rains Retreat.

To mark the end of the Rains Retreat, a ceremony takes place during which Bhikkhus and Bhikkhunis are presented with new Kathina robes. Typically, the robes are dyed pale yellow and made from patches that are sewn together. The story that follows explains the reason for the patches.

The story of the Kathina robe

Thirty Bhikkhus once set out to visit the Buddha. They were hoping to spend the Rains Retreat with him. During the Rains Retreat, Bhikkhus should not travel unless it is strictly necessary. The Rains Retreat began before they could reach the Buddha and so they had to remain where they were for three months. Eventually they were able to continue on their way and at last they caught up with the Buddha. When they told him of their disappointment, he wanted to do something to comfort them. He suggested that they should make a new robe together. People living nearby offered pieces of cloth. The Bhikkhus spread out the pieces of cloth on a frame called a Kathina and shared the task of stitching them together.

Top: *Buddhapada (the Buddha's footprint). Feet represent the grounding of the transcendent. Bodh Gaya, Bihur.* ***Above:*** *The death of Buddha. India, 10th century.*

RITES OF PASSAGE

The only rites of passage performed in Buddhism are the ceremonies associated with initiation into the monastic Sangha and the ceremonies associated with death. Marriage in Buddhist countries is essentially a secular event, although it is usual in Theravada countries for the newly married couple to go to the local temple for a blessing.

INITIATION

A Buddhist cannot be ordained a full member of the Sangha until he or she is 20 years old. However, in Theravada countries such as Thailand and Burma it is customary for boys aged about eleven to spend several months in a monastery, where they receive instruction in the Dhamma (the teaching of the Buddha). In Sri Lanka, once a boy has become a novice monk, he tends to stay a monk for life.

In Thailand, before the boy enters the monastery, his parents shave his head, wash him and dress him in fine clothes reminiscent of those worn by Prince Siddattha. A ceremony then takes place in the home, the purpose of which is to give the boy strength and vitality.

Above: *Image of the Buddha with offerings in a shrine room.*

The following day, now wearing white, he is led in procession to the monastery accompanied by musicians and dancers. At the monastery, he chants his request to become a Bhikkhu (monk) and changes into yellow robes. After agreeing to abide by the full Ten Precepts (see page 4), he is ordained a novice. He is questioned about his wish to become a Bhikkhu and takes a further 227 vows. His family then give him the things that he will need in the monastery. Typically this might be another set of robes, a pair of sandals, some tea, an umbrella, incense, candles and a bowl in which to collect donations of food. Similar initiation ceremonies take place in Burma and Sri Lanka.

DEATH

Beliefs

Buddhists believe in rebirth (see page 6). They believe that when a person dies, the five Khandas (components) that constitute the person break up and are re-constituted in another body. This continues until, after accumulating wisdom through a great number of rebirths, Nibbana is at last attained.

From a Buddhist perspective, everything that exists is impermanent and will ultimately cease to exist. Buddhists therefore adopt an open-minded attitude of acceptance with regard to death.

Customs

Buddhists cremate their dead. Sometimes the funeral pyre is covered with a paper Stupa (see page 10). The mourners wear white, food is eaten and music is played.

Prior to the cremation, a Bhikkhu (monk) preaches a sermon, typically based on the themes of impermanence and rebirth. The mourners are also reminded of the Tiratana (the *Triple Refuge*–see page 3) and of the Five Precepts (see page 4).

PLACES OF WORSHIP

THE VIHARA

The Theravada term Vihara can be used to refer to a monastery, a temple or a shrine room. The Tibetan equivalent is a Gompa. A Vihara consists of a group of buildings or a set of rooms within a single building.

The focus of the shrine room is a raised platform supporting an image of the Buddha. The large central image is usually surrounded by other images. In front of the images are placed offerings of flowers, light, incense, water, and food such as rice and fruit. These are arranged in a way that sets out to achieve a beautiful and calming effect.

When Buddhists honour the image of the Buddha in their worship, they are not worshipping the Buddha as such. Rather, they are worshipping their own potential for enlightenment, as well as offering thanks to the Buddha.

The shrine room will often be used for meditation, but sometimes there is a separate meditation room. This is simpler and less colourful than the shrine room, with a calm and uncluttered atmosphere.

RELIC MOUNDS

Relics of the Buddha were placed under earth mounds which evolved into large, bell-shaped shrines. In India these shrines are called Stupas; in Sri Lanka they are called Dagobas; in Tibet they are called Chortens or Caityas; in Thailand they are called Wats; and in Burma and eastern countries they are called Pagodas. Generally speaking, as Buddhism spread eastwards, the taller and more slender the shrines became.

Early Indian stupa
Stupa I, Sanchi
3rd century BCE

Sri Lankan dagoba
Thuparama
Anuradhapura

Tibetan chorten
Gyantse

Thai wat
Wat Suan Dork
Chiang Mai

Burmese pagoda
Ananda Temple
Pagan Burma
c.1000 CE

Chinese pagoda
Ling-yen-sse
8th century

THE BODHI TREE

Siddattha was sitting under a tree when he achieved enlightenment and became the Buddha (see page 1). This tree later became known as the Bodhi tree (*the Tree of Enlightenment* or *Awakening*). In many places, trees have been grown from cuttings taken from the original tree in Bodh Gaya (*the Place of Enlightenment* or *Awakening*). Places where the descendants of the original tree grow are often important Buddhist shrines and centres of pilgrimage.

RITUAL OBJECTS AND ARTEFACTS

IMAGES OF THE BUDDHA

Buddhist temples and many Buddhist homes contain shrines with images of the Buddha. The images are treated with great respect and are used as aids to meditation and worship.

Statues and pictures of the Buddha depict him in many different ways, each one of which conveys a different aspect of Buddhist teaching. The Buddha is usually shown sitting and meditating or teaching. The different Mudras (hand gestures) have different meanings.

Mudras left to right: *Abhaya (do not fear); Dhyana (meditation); Dharmacakra (preaching, associated with Buddha's first sermon – 'the turning of the wheel of the law'); Bhumisparsa (earth-touching – calling the earth to witness just before the enlightenment at Bodh Gaya).*

IMAGES OF BODHISATTVAS (see page 6)

Avalokiteshvara
There are 108 manifestations of Avalokiteshvara in Nepal alone. He is usually shown either sitting on or stepping down from a lotus throne. He is often depicted with many arms, each one offering a helping hand.

Manjugosha or Manjushri
Manjugosha or Manjushri is generally shown as a young prince with orange-coloured skin. He is usually depicted sitting on a blue lotus. In one hand he wields a sword, symbolic of wisdom, and in the other he carries the Dhamma.

Vajrapani
There are two forms of Vajrapani: a peaceful one and a wrathful one. In his wrathful form he is powerful and terrible in appearance. His skin is blue, he wears a tiger skin around his waist, there are skulls in his hair and he is surrounded by a circle of flames. In one hand he wields the Vajra (the symbolic thunderbolt) from which he gets his name.

Tara
Tara appears in 21 different forms in various colours, of which the White and Green are the oldest. In her Green form she is depicted as a beautiful princess surrounded by a rainbow. She sits in meditation, but one foot is extended indicating her willingness to go to the assistance of others.

Above right: *Green Tara. Tibet, 17th century.*
Right: *Avalokiteshvara in his most familiar form.*

THE WHEEL OF LIFE

The Wheel of Life is full of symbolism relating to the Buddha's teaching on impermanence and suffering.

The Wheel is held in the grip of Yama, Lord of Death. In the centre circle (the hub) a cock, a snake and a pig endlessly chase each other, biting each other's tails. The red cock represents passion and lust. The green snake represents hatred and aggression. The black pig represents ignorance and confusion.

The spokes of the Wheel divide up the six realms: those of hell, hungry ghosts, animals, titans, gods and humans.

The outer rim contains twelve images showing people caught up in the chain of cause and effect that is Kamma. Such a chain perpetuates the cycle of life, death and rebirth that is Samsara.

MANDALAS

A Mandala is a geometric pattern (usually circular) which represents a person's world: the outer world of the universe or cosmos and the inner world of the self. Mandalas are used as a focus for meditation. The journey that the meditator makes through the intricate concentric rings to the still centre symbolises a person's spiritual journey to the Absolute Truth. Mandalas are associated with Tibetan Buddhism in particular. They can be painted or painstakingly made from sand or coloured grains of rice.

Right: *Mandala depicting the origin of the cosmos through the evolution of the planets and elements, Pavo Dzong, Bhutan.*

THANKAS

Thankas are pictures painted on cloth surrounded by colourful embroidered patterns.They are popular in Tibet and Bhutan, where they are used as aids to meditation. Images of the Buddha, Bodhisattvas, Buddhist saints, the Wheel of Life and Mandalas all feature on Thankas. Most Thankas are the size of posters, small enough to hang inside a room, but they can be large enough to cover the entire outside wall of a monastery.

PRAYER WHEELS

Prayer wheels are used extensively in Tibetan Buddhism. A prayer wheel comprises a cylindrical barrel containing Mantras written on parchment. The most frequently used Mantra is 'Om mani padme hum' (see page 5).

Prayer wheels can be very large, mounted on walls, or small enough to be hand-held. As the wheel is spun, compassionate thoughts are projected to all sentient beings. Prayer flags, which have Mantras written on them, serve a similar purpose.

PRAYER BEADS

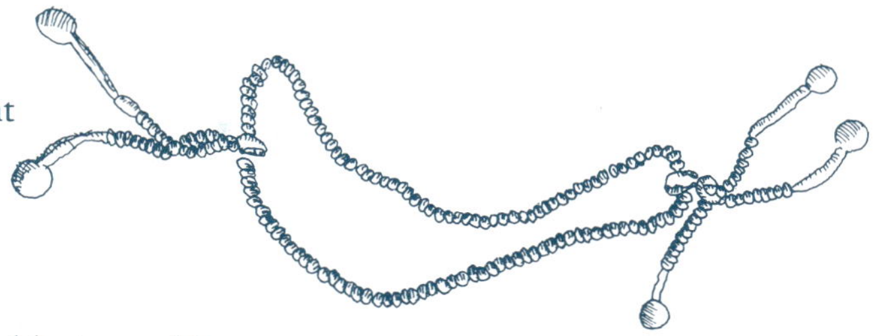

Buddhist prayer beads usually comprise 108 beads strung together in a circle. They are used to keep count when performing prostrations or repeating Mantras (sacred formulae or chants).

DORJE AND BELL

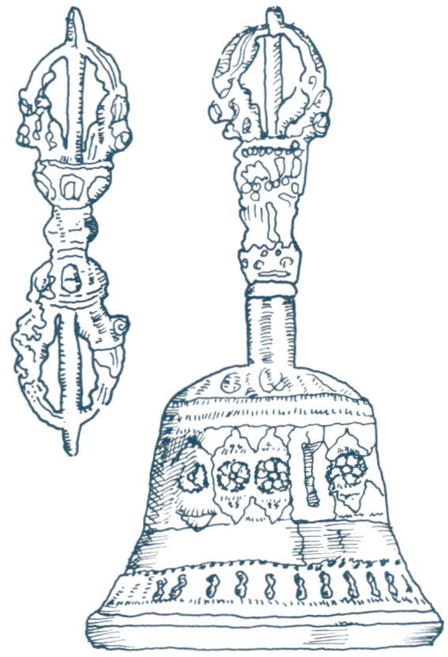

The Dorje and Bell are the two most important ritual objects used in Tantric Buddhism, a form of Buddhism found in Tibet, Bhutan, Ladakh and Nepal. According to Tantric teaching, it is possible to achieve instant enlightenment through the use of rituals, Mantras and Mandalas.

The Dorje (also called the Vajra) represents a thunderbolt. The thunderbolt, with its associations of concentrated power, is a symbol of the moment of instant awakening or enlightenment. The Dorje is thought of as being masculine and is held in the right hand.

The clear sound of the Bell (also called the Ghanta) symbolises wisdom. The Bell is thought of as being feminine and is held in the left hand.

SYMBOLS

THE EIGHT SPOKED WHEEL

The outer rim of the wheel represents Samsara, the seemingly endless cycle of life, death and rebirth. At the still centre of the wheel is Nibbana. The eight spokes, which represent the Noble Eightfold Path, lead from the whirling outer rim to the still centre; from Samsara to Nibbana.

The Buddha's first sermon, which was given in the deer park at the city of Varanasi or Banaras, summarised the main points of his teaching. The sermon is known as 'the turning of the wheel of the law'.

THE LOTUS

The lotus rises from the muddy depths of the pool to open itself up and to float upon the sunlit surface. So human beings have the capacity to rise above the the condition imposed upon them by Samsara and to attain their full flowering in the state that is Nibbana.

Christianity

'LOVE THE LORD YOUR GOD WITH ALL YOUR HEART, WITH ALL YOUR SOUL, WITH ALL YOUR MIND.'
This is the greatest and most important commandment.
The second most important commandment is like it:
'Love your neighbour as you love yourself.'
The whole law of Moses and the teachings of the prophets depend on these two commandments.

Matthew 22. 37–39

BACKGROUND INFORMATION

JESUS

Jesus was born in Bethlehem approximately 2,000 years ago (around 4 BCE). His mother, Mary, was married to a carpenter called Joseph, and he grew up in the town of Nazareth.

When he was about 30, Jesus was baptised in the River Jordan by John the Baptist. This proved to be a turning-point in his life. The baptism experience confirmed his special relationship with God. It became clear to Jesus that God wanted him to devote the rest of his life to proclaiming the Gospel (*the Good News*):

The Spirit of the Lord is upon me, because he has chosen me to bring good news to the poor. He has sent me to proclaim liberty to the captives and recovery of sight to the blind; to set free the oppressed and announce that the time has come when the Lord will save his people. (Luke 4.18-19)

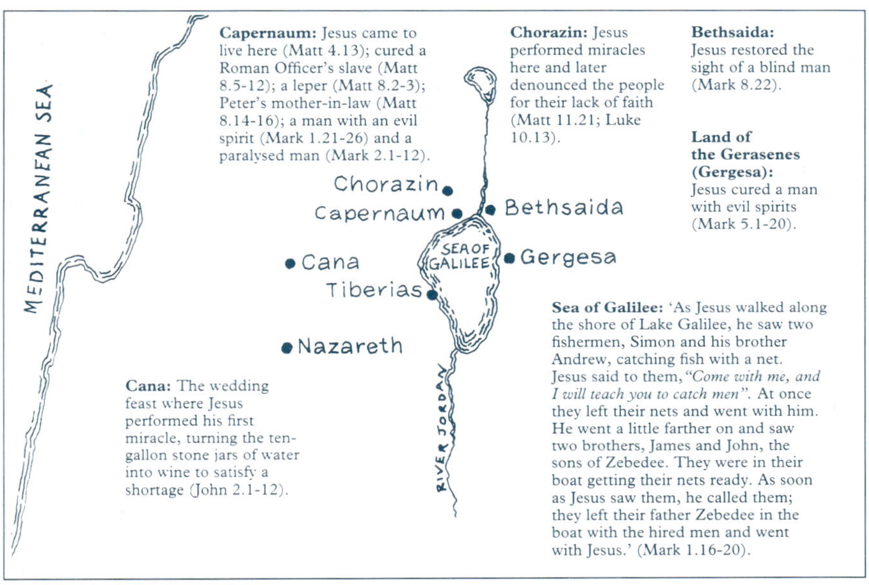

ORIGINS

Jesus of Nazareth or Jesus Christ (the founder of Christianity) was a Jewish teacher who lived in a Roman province comprising part of present-day Israel. He lived early in the first century CE. His followers were initially all Jews, and many of them believed him to be the promised Messiah of Jewish tradition. Christians regard Jesus as the Son of God.

Note: All Biblical quotations are taken from the Good News Bible.

For the next three years, until his crucifixion, Jesus travelled around teaching and healing. His mission started in Galilee, where he chose twelve men (known as apostles) to be his travelling companions and assistants. The apostles are sometimes referred to as the twelve disciples.

The stories that Jesus told (called parables) and the miracles that he performed served to illustrate the nature and meaning of the Kingdom of God. This spiritual kingdom, ruled over by God, would be established on earth bringing with it peace, harmony, justice and love.

The concept of love was central to the teachings of Jesus. For Jesus, the two greatest commandments were:

Love the Lord your God with all your heart, with all your soul, and with all your mind... (and) love your neighbour as you love yourself. (Matthew 22.37-39)

Above: *The calling of Peter and Andrew, Italy, 520* CE.

Jesus' teachings and actions were seen as a challenge by both religious and political authorities. At the time of the Passover festival, when Jewish nationalistic feelings tended to run high, Jesus rode into Jerusalem through cheering crowds. The authorities, fearing an insurrection, decided that it was time to act. After eating the 'last supper' with the apostles (the meal at which the Eucharist was inaugurated – see page 26), Jesus was betrayed by Judas Iscariot and arrested in the Garden of Gethsemane. The Roman Governor, Pontius Pilate, eventually ordered his execution. Jesus was crucified at Golgotha around the year 29 CE.

Christians believe that after his death, Jesus was resurrected by God and that he appeared to the apostles and to some of his friends. When the apostles and other disciples gathered to celebrate the feast of Pentecost, they were filled with the power of the Holy Spirit. This provided the impetus for them to carry Jesus' message across the world.

PAUL

The most influential of the early Christian missionaries was Paul, originally called Saul. He was a Jew from the city of Tarsus and was well versed in rabbinic teaching. At first he vigorously persecuted Christians, but after a profound religious experience on the road to Damascus, he converted to Christianity and changed his name to Paul. He made three major missionary journeys, establishing groups of Christians in present-day Turkey and Greece. He was the first to encourage non-Jews to become Christians. The letters or epistles that he wrote to the early Christian communities are an important source of theological truths for Christians.

Above: *Saint Paul preaching to the Thessalonians.*

THE CHURCH

For a long period, Christians in the Roman Empire were persecuted and many thousands were martyred, but eventually (beginning with the conversion of the Emperor Constantine) Christianity became the official religion of the Roman Empire. When the Roman Empire became divided into Western and Eastern parts, Christianity split into the Western Church (embracing Roman Catholicism) and the Eastern Church (embracing Eastern Orthodoxy).

During the Reformation of the sixteenth and seventeenth centuries, the Western Church experienced lasting internal divisions caused by the emergence of Protestantism. During the reign of Henry VIII, the Church of England was established. Other Protestant Christian traditions represented in Britain today include the Scottish Presbyterian, Baptist, Methodist and United Reform Churches.

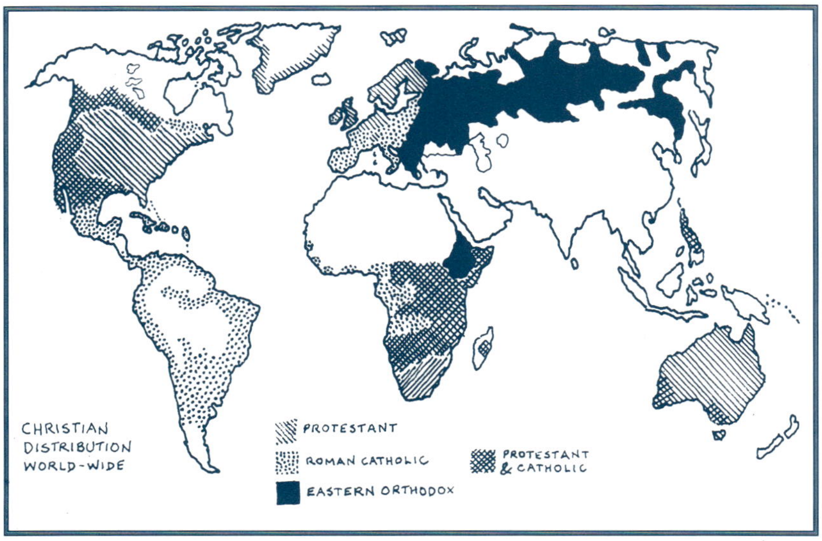

CHRISTIANS TODAY

With around 1,800 million followers worldwide, Christianity in its many and diverse forms is the largest of the world's religions. It is also the principal religious tradition of Great Britain (in terms of numbers of adherents, historical presence and cultural influence). There are nearly 40 million Christians in Britain, the majority of whom belong to the Church of England.

BELIEFS AND WAY OF LIFE

THE NICENE CREED

Christianity has experienced many conflicts of belief during the 2,000 years of its existence. Despite these conflicts, there are certain basic beliefs to which all Christians adhere. In 325 CE, at a time when internal divisions and differences of belief were posing a serious threat to the unity of the Church, the Council of Nicea attempted to arrive at an agreed summary of the principal Christian beliefs. A basic statement of Christian beliefs, known as the Apostles' Creed (from the Latin 'credo' which means 'I believe'), had been in existence since the year 110 CE. The Council of Nicea developed the Apostles' Creed into the Nicene Creed, which most Christians in the world today still accept. The version of the Nicene creed currently used by Anglicans and Roman Catholics is as follows:

We believe in one God, the Father, the almighty, maker of heaven and earth, of all that is, seen and unseen. We believe in one Lord, Jesus Christ, the only begotten Son of God, eternally begotten of the Father, God from God, Light from Light, true God from true God, begotten not made, of one being with the Father. Through him all things were made. For us men and for our salvation he came down from heaven; by the power of the Holy Spirit he became incarnate by the Virgin Mary, and was made man. For our sake he was crucified under Pontius Pilate, he suffered death and was buried. On the third day he rose again in accordance with the Scriptures; he ascended into heaven and is seated at the right hand of the Father. He will come again in glory to judge the living and the dead, and his kingdom will have no end. We believe in the Holy Spirit, the Lord, the giver of life, who proceeds from the Father and the Son. With the Father and the Son he is worshipped and glorified. He has spoken through the prophets. We believe in one holy catholic and apostolic Church. We acknowledge one baptism for the forgiveness of sins. We look for the resurrection of the dead, and the life of the world to come. Amen.

Some of the main beliefs expressed in the Nicene Creed are the Creation, the Trinity, the Incarnation and the Resurrection.

Above: *Symbols of the Trinity.*
Below: *The bursting pomegranate, the phoenix and the butterfly. Symbols of the resurrection.*

THE TRINITY

One of the most mysterious and paradoxical of Christian beliefs is that of the Trinity. Christians profess that there is only one God, but that this God is 'Three in One' and 'One in Three'. Christians speak of God as Father, Son and Holy Spirit:

> ***God the Father*** *is the creator of everything that exists.*
> ***God the Son*** *is Jesus, in whom God became fully human and appeared on this earth.*
> ***God the Holy Spirit*** *is active in the world as divine energy which touches people in their daily lives.*

THE INCARNATION

Christians believe that, paradoxically, Jesus was both fully human and fully divine. The belief that God became a human being in the person of Jesus is known as the Incarnation. Through Jesus, the essential nature of God is revealed as being that of self-giving love.

THE RESURRECTION

The self-giving love of Jesus is most fully expressed in his death. Through the lonely agony of his crucifixion, Jesus experienced the worst of human suffering. However, Christians believe that through the Resurrection (the raising of Jesus from the dead), Jesus overcame the power of death and achieved absolute freedom for himself and for those who put their trust in him.

Christians believe that sin separates people from God. This idea, contained originally in the story of Adam and Eve (Genesis 2 and 3), has traditionally been expressed in the doctrines of the Fall and Original Sin. Sin in this context can be defined as an act of rebellion or disobedience to the known will of God.

By going willingly to the cross, Jesus paid for human mistakes, making up for people's misuse of the freedom which God has given them. By defeating death, Jesus achieved an Atonement (at-one-ment): a reconciliation between God and humankind, a restoration of the relationship broken by sin.

VALUES

The Christian way of life is characterised at least as much by adherence to a general ethical code as by observance of religious rituals and practices. Jesus spoke harshly of those who merely observed the outward forms of religion without living out the love of God and of others in their daily lives. Jesus had a particular concern for the poor, the disadvantaged and social outcasts, and many Christians find practical expression of their religious commitment in caring for others, in performing charity work and in supporting worthwhile social causes.

WRITINGS

Above: *Resurrection, Germany, 1512CE.*
Below: *The Bible.*

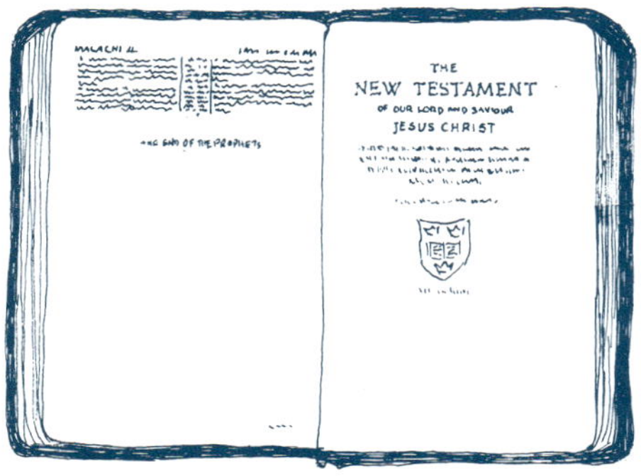

THE BIBLE

All Christians accept the authority of the Bible, although there have always been differences in the way that the Bible is interpreted. Today, there are Christians who believe that the words of the Bible are true in a literal sense, while others regard Bible stories as essentially symbolic or allegorical expressions of profound spiritual insights.

The Bible is not one continuous narrative. It is a collection of sixty-six separate books contained in a single volume. Many of the books originated in oral tradition stretching back over thousands of years. The origins, authorship and purpose of the books are wide-ranging. The rich and diverse literary styles contained within the Bible include myth, legend, history, poetry, song, proverb, story, parable and epistle. The many literary forms of the Bible include symbol, allegory, analogy, simile and metaphor.

The Bible is divided into two sections, known as the Old and New Testaments. The Old Testament relates the ancient history of the Jewish people. The New Testament provides various accounts of the teaching and activities of Jesus and tells the early history of the Christian Church.

The Old Testament contains thirty-nine books, the contents of which make up the Tenakh (the Jewish Bible).

THE NEW TESTAMENT

The New Testament contains twenty-seven books, including the four Gospels which are by far the most important books of the Bible for Christians.

The Gospels contain the main records of the life and teaching of Jesus, but they were not written as biographical accounts. Rather, they were written to record and proclaim the Good News that the Kingdom of God had come in Christ (Gospel means 'Good News').

Mark's Gospel was the first to be written. It was written around 70 CE, some forty years after the death of Jesus. The Gospels of Matthew and Luke share much of the same material as that of Mark, and these three (Matthew, Mark and Luke) are known as the Synoptic Gospels. John's Gospel, the last to be written, is very different in style and contains much that is not found in any of the other Gospels.

The Gospels are followed by the Acts of the Apostles, written by the Gospel writer Luke. Acts provides an account of the actions of the first Christians (including Paul) after the death and resurrection of Jesus.

There are twenty-one letters or epistles in the New Testament, mostly written by Paul (see page 16), giving advice and guidance to the early Christian communities.

The remaining book of the New Testament, Revelation, contains an extraordinary, apocalyptic vision of the end of the world, full of vivid symbolism and imagery. The book ends with a dazzling picture of the new heaven and new earth that will be established with God's Kingdom.

Above: *Joseph and Mary heed the angel's warning. 'Herod will be looking for the child in order to kill him. So get up, take the child and his mother and escape to Egypt.'* (Matthew 2.13)

FESTIVALS

ADVENT (November-December)

Advent is the period, lasting about four weeks, which precedes Christmas. Advent candles, calendars and wreaths (see page 29) are used to mark the days and weeks leading up to Christmas. During Advent, Christmas cards are sent to friends and relatives, and nativity plays are often performed in schools.

As Christmas approaches, carol services are held in churches, often incorporating nine lessons or readings taken from the Bible. The lessons culminate in the story of the birth of Jesus.

During the week before Christmas, many churches hold Christingle services. This custom originated in America. During the service, children hold lighted Christingles in a darkened church (see page 29).

Note: Certain Orthodox Churches follow the Julian calendar, which in the twentieth century operates thirteen days behind the Gregorian calendar. The Gregorian calendar is much more widely used, and the festival dates in this publication are given in accordance with the Gregorian calendar.

CHRISTMAS (25 December-6 January)

Christmas is a twelve-day celebration of the birth of Jesus. Throughout the twelve days, homes are filled with decorations, many of which have pre-Christian origins. The candles and lights are a reminder that 25 December, occurring just after the midwinter solstice, was the day on which Romans celebrated the rebirth of Sol Invictus (*the Unconquerable Sun*). Evergreens were used to decorate homes during Teutonic midwinter rituals, which included the lighting of the Yule log. St Francis of Assisi constructed the first Christmas crib in 1223 CE.

The Christmas festival starts on Christmas Day (25 December), and many Christians attend a midnight service, such as Midnight Mass, on Christmas Eve. Various customs are associated with Christmas Day: children receive gifts from Father Christmas or Santa Claus (St Nicholas); presents are exchanged; and families come together to eat a traditional meal, which in Britain usually includes roast turkey and Christmas pudding.

EPIPHANY (6 January)

Epiphany marks the end of the twelve days of Christmas. Traditionally all Christmas decorations are taken down on Twelfth Night. In the Western Church, Epiphany commemorates the adoration of the Magi (the three kings of popular tradition), who honoured the baby Jesus with their gifts of gold, frankincense and myrrh.

CANDLEMAS (2 February)

Candlemas commemorates the presentation of the infant Jesus in the Temple in Jerusalem. In many churches a candle-lit procession recalls Simeon's words to Mary and Joseph, when he describes Jesus as a light to reveal God to the nations of the world.

Above: *Jesus is tempted by the Devil. 'The Devil took Jesus to a very high mountain and showed him all the kingdoms of the world in all their greatness.'* (Matthew 4.8)
Below: *Jesus enters Jerusalem on a donkey, Albani Psalter, 12th century.*

SHROVE TUESDAY AND ASH WEDNESDAY (February)

These days are a time of preparation for Lent. Shrove Tuesday is more commonly known as Pancake Day because on this day it used to be the custom to make pancakes out of foods being given up for Lent, foods such as eggs, milk and flour which were once considered luxuries. In French-speaking countries, Shrove Tuesday is called Mardi Gras and it is characterised by carnival processions: a chance for festive self-indulgence prior to the austerities of Lent.

Ash Wednesday, which follows Shrove Tuesday, marks the beginning of Lent. It is so called because in some churches there is a ceremony during which the priest marks each worshipper's forehead with the sign of the cross in ash, reminding them of their mortality. The ash used often comes from palm crosses kept from the previous year and burned.

LENT (February-March/April)

During the forty days of Lent, Christians remember the forty days that Jesus spent in the wilderness during which he was tempted by Satan. Lent is a time of penitence and self-sacrifice. Many Christians try to give up certain luxuries and indulgences during this time.

HOLY WEEK (March/April)

Holy Week is the last week of Lent. During Holy Week, Christians remember the suffering and death of Jesus.

PALM SUNDAY

Palm Sunday is the first day of Holy Week. It commemorates the entry of Jesus into Jerusalem, when he rode on a donkey and was welcomed by people waving palm fronds. In many churches, palm crosses are given out (see page 29), and there may also be processions.

MAUNDY THURSDAY

Maundy Thursday is the day when Christians commemorate the Last Supper. Maundy comes from the Latin word 'mandatum', which means commandment. At the Last Supper, as a sign of humility, Jesus washed the feet of his disciples and told them to do the same for each other.

GOOD FRIDAY

On Good Friday, the day on which hot cross buns are traditionally eaten, Christians recall the crucifixion of Jesus. It is a solemn and an austere day, during which Christians meditate on the sufferings of Jesus. In Roman Catholic churches, which are stripped of the usual decorations, people contemplate the Stations of the Cross (see page 25). In Orthodox churches, the priest lowers an icon depicting the dead Christ while members of the congregation stand with lighted candles just as they would at a funeral.

HOLY SATURDAY

No special activities take place on Holy Saturday, the last day of Lent, until the evening. In many churches there is an evening service which starts in darkness. The worshippers light candles from the Paschal candle (see page 29) and the church gradually fills with light. This symbolises the triumph of life over death and the victory of good over evil, themes that will be taken up during the Easter Day celebrations which follow. During the service, baptismal vows are renewed in preparation for Easter.

Above: *Jesus is executed as a common criminal. 'Jesus said, "Forgive them, Father! They don't know what they are doing."'* (Luke 23.34)

EASTER DAY (March/April)

In the West, the commercialism that surrounds Christmas makes it easy to forget that Easter Sunday is the most important day of the Christian year. On Easter Day, Christians celebrate the resurrection of Jesus. It is a joyful occasion on which many people make a special effort to go to church. Many of the symbols used in Easter celebrations, such as Easter eggs, are associated with new life and the coming of Spring.

ASCENSION DAY (May)

Ascension Day occurs forty days after Easter and commemorates Jesus' ascension into heaven.

WHITSUN (May)

The name Whitsun derives from White Sunday, when the newly baptised dressed in white. Whitsun is the popular name for Pentecost, which is itself an alternative name for the Jewish festival of Shavuot. After Jesus' ascension, the apostles were gathered together for Pentecost when they received the gift of the Holy Spirit. There was a rushing wind, tongues of fire appeared and they spoke in different languages. This marked the beginning of the Christian Church.

Above: *The apostles are filled with the power of the Holy Spirit at Pentecost. 'They saw what looked like tongues of fire which spread out and touched each person there.'* (Acts 2.3)

RITES OF PASSAGE

BIRTH

Infant Baptism

All churches have ceremonies welcoming babies into the Christian community. The ceremony may take the form of a service of Infant Dedication but in the majority of churches, including the Church of England, the Roman Catholic Church and the Orthodox Churches, it takes the form of a service of baptism. Baptisms are popularly known as Christenings. The word Christening comes from 'Christ-naming', because this is the occasion when the baby is given publicly her/his 'Christian' name.

For baptism, the baby is dressed in a white Christening gown (symbolic of purity). In Anglican and Roman Catholic churches, parents, godparents, friends and relatives gather around the font. The parents and godparents declare their intention to nurture the child in the Christian faith and the godparents take vows on the baby's behalf. The priest asks the parents to name the child, then, using a hand or a scallop shell, pours water from the font three times onto the baby's head, baptising her/him in the name of the Father, the Son and the Holy Spirit. The water is a symbol of rebirth and cleansing. A lighted candle may be given to the parents or godparents (see page 29), and the sign of the cross is made on the baby's forehead. In Roman Catholic baptisms, the child is anointed on the chest with oil of baptism and on the head with oil of chrism.

Above: *Baptism at a church font.*
Below: *Jesus is baptised by John in the river Jordan. 'Then heaven was opened to him, and he saw the Spirit of God coming down like a dove and alighting on him. Then a voice said from heaven, "This is my own dear Son, with whom I am pleased."'* (Matthew 3.16-17)

In Orthodox baptisms, whether for infants or adults, the whole person is immersed in water three times. This signifies belief in the Trinity, the death of past sins, and new life in Jesus. Baptism is immediately followed by Chrismation, during which forehead, eyelids, nose, mouth, ears, chest, hands and feet are anointed with special oil or ointment, blessed beforehand by a Bishop. In the Orthodox Churches there is no equivalent of confirmation. Once a child has been baptised and anointed with sacred chrism, she/he can receive Holy Communion.

COMING OF AGE

Adult or Believer's Baptism

Baptists believe that baptism involves making a personal commitment to Christ, which children are too young to make. In the Baptist Church, therefore, only adults are baptised. This is done by total immersion in a pool situated inside the church in front of the congregation.

First Communion and Confirmation

In order to become a full member of the Church of England or the Roman Catholic Church, a person must publicly 'confirm' the promises made on her/his behalf at baptism. In the Roman Catholic Church it is customary for children to receive their first Communion when they are about eight years old, several years before they are confirmed. For First Communion girls wear white dresses and white veils over their heads.

Before the service of confirmation, the candidates (usually aged between eleven and the early teens) attend confirmation classes, during which they receive instruction in the teachings of the Church. The service is conducted by a bishop, who asks the candidates to affirm their belief in the Christian faith. He then places his hands on the head of each candidate as she/he kneels before him and asks God to 'confirm' that person with the Holy Spirit. An additional feature of confirmation services in the Roman Catholic Church is that the bishop uses holy chrism to make the sign of the cross on the forehead of each candidate.

MARRIAGE

Christians regard marriage as a lifelong commitment, one of the main purposes of which is the procreation and upbringing of children. For Roman Catholics, marriage is a sacrament and divorce is not permissible.

In England, on the three Sundays preceding the wedding, banns are read out in church to make sure that there is no reason why the couple should not be married. The marriage service is similar in Anglican and Roman Catholic churches. The bride traditionally wears white (symbolic of purity) and carries a bouquet of flowers. She is attended by bridesmaids and is 'given away' by her father. In front of family and friends, the couple exchange marriage vows and rings, which are blessed by the priest. After the ceremony, outside the church, confetti and rice are thrown.

In Orthodox churches, after exchanging vows and rings, the couple are crowned with coronets or garlands and drink wine from the same cup. Finally the priest leads them in a circular procession, indicating that the marriage will have no end. Despite this, Orthodox Churches permit divorce if things go very wrong and allow re-marriage in church.

Above: *A bridal couple.*

DEATH

Beliefs

Christians believe that there is an afterlife, but there is disagreement as to its nature. Some Christians believe that as soon as a person dies, she/he is judged by God and the person's soul goes immediately to Heaven or Hell. Many Roman Catholics believe in Purgatory, where an impure soul resides until it is fit to enter Heaven. Other Christians believe that the soul stays with the body until the Day of Judgement, when the dead will return to life to be judged by God and the world will end.

Customs

When a Christian dies, the body is placed in a wooden coffin. Orthodox Christians are covered in a burial shroud which has pictures of the crucifixion (in black) and the resurrection (in red) printed on it. The funeral service takes place in a church or a crematorium chapel. If the body is buried, there is a service of committal at the graveside.

If the body is cremated, the ashes may be buried in a grave some time later or scattered in a place which has special associations for the dead person.

Right: *A burial shroud used by Orthodox Christians.*

PLACES OF WORSHIP

Christians use a great variety of buildings as places of worship, including private houses, churches, cathedrals, abbeys, minsters, chapels and citadels (used by members of the Salvation Army). The main features of some of these buildings are described below.

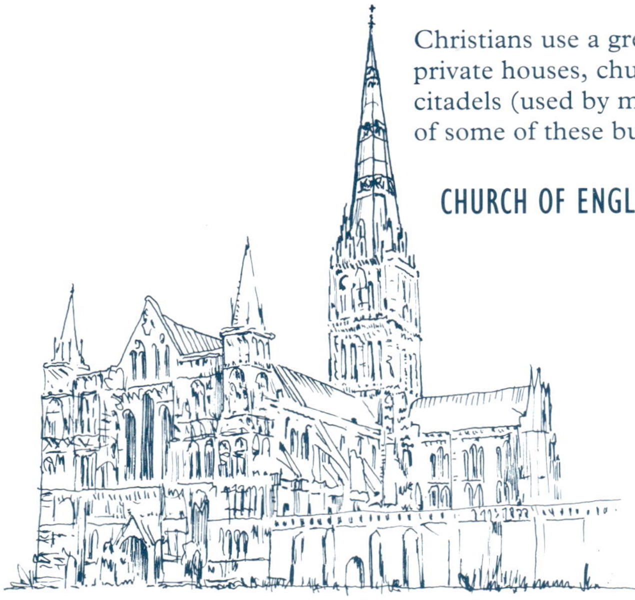

CHURCH OF ENGLAND CHURCHES

Anglican churches are traditionally built in the shape of a cross with a tower or steeple, although modern churches often break away from the traditional design. The congregation sits in the nave (the main body of the church) facing east, towards the Holy Land. The east end of the church usually narrows into the chancel, where the choir sits. At the east end there is also an altar which represents the table used by Jesus and the disciples at the Last Supper. A cross and candles are often placed on the altar which is covered in an altar cloth.

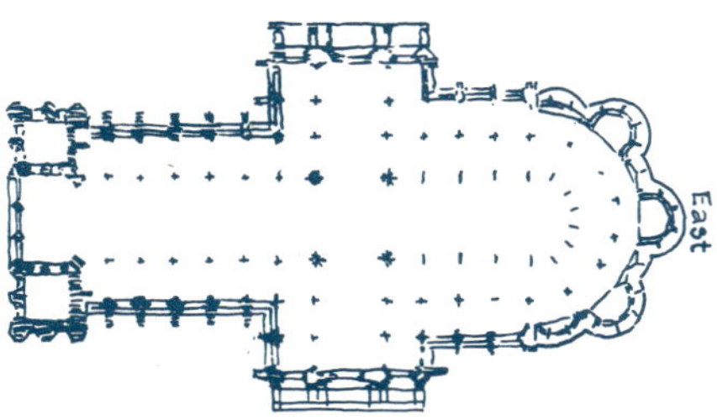

The font, which is a basin or bowl on a pedestal containing water for baptism, is usually found near the main entrance (baptism marks a person's entry into the Christian Church). The pulpit, from which the sermon is preached, and the lectern, from which the Bible is read out, generally stand on either side of the nave at the point where it meets the chancel. The lectern is sometimes shaped like an eagle with outstretched wings. An organ usually provides the music.

ROMAN CATHOLIC CHURCHES

Roman Catholic churches usually share all the features of Anglican churches that have just been described. Additional features common to Roman Catholic churches, but which are also found in some Church of England churches (especially Anglo-Catholic churches), include the stoup, the tabernacle, devotional statues, the Stations of the Cross, confessionals and the Lady Chapel.

The stoup is a small basin containing holy water that is situated just inside the main entrance. Upon entering the church, worshippers dip their fingertips into the water and cross themselves. They may also genuflect (bow down on one knee) towards the altar.

The tabernacle is a cupboard or safe made out of cloth to resemble a tent. It contains the reserved sacrament, that is bread or wafers that have already been consecrated ready for Mass. A light is constantly kept burning in front of the Tabernacle to symbolise the eternal presence of God.

The most popular of the devotional statues is invariably that of Mary, the mother of Jesus. Her statue is often surrounded by candles lit by people praying for her to intercede on their behalf.

Top: *Salisbury Cathedral, 1220-60 CE, a fine example of a Gothic church.*
Centre: *The floor plans of many churches represent the cross on which Jesus died.*
Bottom: *Statue of Virgin and Child, Notre Dame, Paris, 14th century.*

The ***Stations of the Cross*** comprise fourteen carved or painted pictures depicting the events leading up to and immediately following the crucifixion. They are arranged in sequence around the interior walls of the church.

Confessionals used for the Sacrament of Penance or Reconciliation, are either a small room or two cubicles linked by a grille so that anonymity may be assured. The priest sits on one side and listens to the confessions made by the person kneeling on the other side.

The ***Lady Chapel*** is a side chapel dedicated to Mary, the mother of Jesus. It is used for personal prayer and meditation.

ORTHODOX CHURCHES

Orthodox churches are usually built in the shape of a cross with arms of equal length and with a dome above the centre. One of the arms is partitioned off from the rest of the church by a screen called the Iconostasis. The Iconostasis, the interior of the dome and all the walls are covered in icons (see page 28) depicting Jesus, Mary and various saints. The icons vary in size but they are all painted according to the same conventions.

In the middle of the Iconostasis there is a door covered by a scarlet curtain. The curtain represents the curtain of the Temple in Jerusalem, and only priests may go beyond it. At certain points during services, the curtain is drawn back and the door is opened to reveal the holy table or throne, which symbolises the presence of God. Behind this stands the Bishop's throne. During services, men and women stand separately. All the singing is unaccompanied. Usually there is a choir, which stands out of sight of the congregation.

BAPTIST CHAPELS

A Baptist chapel is dominated by the pulpit, which stands at one end and from which the minister conducts the service. Set into the floor in front of the pulpit is a rectangular baptismal pool where Believers' Baptisms are performed for adults wanting to become full members of the Baptist Church.

RELIGIOUS SOCIETY OF FRIENDS' (QUAKERS') MEETING HOUSES

Meeting Houses are very plain and simple, usually comprising a sparsely furnished room, empty apart from a table and a few chairs. On the table there is a copy of the Bible and possibly some flowers. Meetings are spent in quiet reflection. People sit in a silence that is unbroken except for occasional readings and the sharing of personal experiences and thoughts.

SALVATION ARMY HALLS OR CITADELS

The Salvation Army Hall (often known as The Citadel) is the local base for this international evangelical church. The central feature of the Hall is the Mercy Seat: a wooden bench where people can have communion with God. The Mercy Seat is available for use by individuals at any time, including during services. Music plays an important part in Salvation Army services and praise, and features prominently in street meetings.

Above: *Three of the Stations of the Cross.*

i Jesus is condemned to death
ii Jesus receives the cross
iii Jesus falls the first time
iv Jesus is met by Mary his mother
v The cross is laid on Simon of Cyrenae
vi Veronica wipes the face of Jesus
vii Jesus falls a second time
viii The women of Jerusalem mourn for Jesus
ix Jesus falls a third time
x Jesus is stripped of his clothes
xi Jesus is nailed to the cross
xii Jesus dies on the cross
xiii Jesus is taken down from the cross
xiv Jesus is placed in the tomb.

THE EUCHARIST

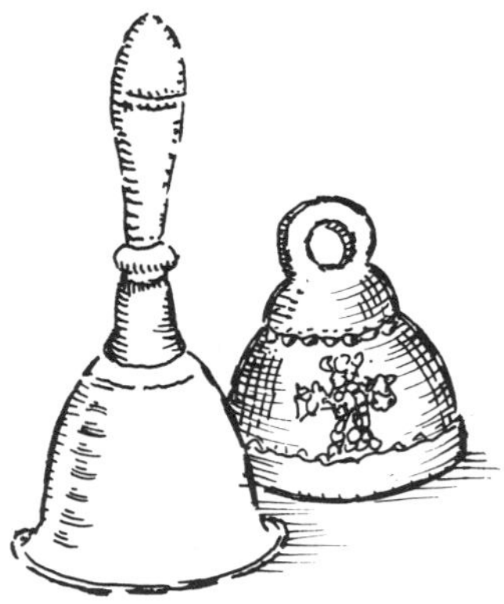

***Above:** A bell, rung during the church service to draw attention to parts of the service.*

Sunday is the day set aside for Christian worship, and for most Christians the most important church service is the Eucharist (*the thanksgiving meal*). The Eucharist is also known as Holy Communion (among Anglicans), Mass (among Roman Catholics), the Lord's Supper and the Breaking of Bread. It commemorates the Last Supper, when Jesus shared bread and wine with the apostles, saying that they were his body and blood. The Last Supper, which took place on the night that Jesus was arrested, is thought by many to have been the Seder meal, comprising part of the Jewish festival of Pesach (see Judaism section page 80).

Different Churches celebrate the Eucharist in different ways. In the Church of England, bread (often in the form of a wafer) is eaten and a sip of red wine is taken. Roman Catholics believe in transubstantiation. That is that at the words of consecration, the substance of the bread and wine actually becomes the substance of the body and blood of Jesus. In Orthodox Churches bread is dipped in wine and offered to each person on a long-handled spoon. In Protestant Churches such as the Baptist Church and the United Reformed Church, the wine is usually distributed in small individual cups.

The Orthodox Church is the only Church which allows small children to participate fully in the Eucharist. In the Church of England, a person must be confirmed before being able to receive Holy Communion. In the Roman Catholic Church, children receive their First Communion before they are confirmed.

Two Christian denominations which do not celebrate the Eucharist are the Religious Society of Friends (sometimes referred to as the Quakers) and the Salvation Army.

SACRAMENTS

A sacrament can be defined as an outward and visible sign of an inward blessing. Protestants recognise two sacraments: Eucharist (see above) and baptism (see page 22). Roman Catholics recognise five more: confirmation, penance, marriage, ordination to the priesthood and anointing the sick with oil.

THE LORD'S PRAYER

***Above:** The priest breaks the Host while recalling the events of the Last Supper.*

The prayer that Jesus taught his disciples (see for instance Matthew 6.9-13) has always been an important feature of Christian worship. The version that the Church of England currently uses is as follows:

Our father in heaven,
hallowed be your name,
your kingdom come,
your will be done,
on earth as in heaven.
Give us today our daily bread.
Forgive us our sins
as we forgive those who sin against us.
Lead us not into temptation
but deliver us from evil.
For the kingdom, the power and the glory are yours
now and forever. Amen.

PRIESTS, BISHOPS, etc

In the Church of England, priests may be men or women and they are allowed to be married. In the Roman Catholic and Orthodox Churches, only men can be ordained priests. Once a man has been ordained in either the Roman Catholic or the Orthodox Churches, he is not permitted to marry.

The reigning British monarch is head of the Church of England, but its leader in effect is the Archbishop of Canterbury. Next in importance to the Archbishop of Canterbury is the Archbishop of York. Under the Archbishops come the Bishops, most of whom are in charge of a diocese. Within each diocese there are many parishes, each with its parish priest or vicar. Parish priests are often be helped in their work by assistant priests called curates.

The head of the Roman Catholic Church is the Pope, who lives in the Vatican city in Rome. His chief counsellors are the Cardinals, and it is the Cardinals who elect a new Pope when the existing one dies.

RITUAL OBJECTS AND ARTEFACTS

CROSSES

Latin Cross
The Latin cross is a plain cross without the figure of Jesus on it, to commemorate the risen Jesus.

Crucifix
A crucifix is a cross which has the figure of Jesus attached to it.

Rosary
A rosary consists of a string of beads with a crucifix attached. Rosaries are used by some Roman Catholics as aids to prayer. Starting at the crucifix, the beads are passed between thumb and forefinger as the worshipper 'says the rosary'. The beads help the worshipper to concentrate and to remember the set sequence of prayers, which includes the 'Our Father', the 'Hail Mary' and the 'Glory Be'.

During each circuit of the rosary, the worshipper meditates on a set of five mysteries. The five Joyful Mysteries are associated with happy events in Jesus' early life. The five Sorrowful Mysteries are associated with the sad events at the end of Jesus' life. The five Glorious Mysteries are associated with the wonderful things that are believed to have happened after Jesus and Mary died.

The 'Hail Mary'

Hail Mary, full of grace,
The Lord is with thee.
Blessed art thou among women,
and blessed is the fruit of thy womb,
Jesus.
Holy Mary, Mother of God,
pray for us sinners now
and at the hour of our death. Amen.

The 'Glory Be'

Glory be to the Father,
and to the Son,
and to the Holy Spirit,
As it was in the beginning,
is now and ever shall be,
world without end. Amen.

Other Crosses

There are many other forms of the cross, including the Russian Orthodox cross, which has three cross-beams representing (from top to bottom) the notice nailed above Jesus' head, the beam to which Jesus' arms were nailed and a smaller, slanting beam which supported his feet; the Greek cross, which has arms of equal length; and the Celtic cross, which has a circle symbolising eternity at the intersection of the vertical and horizontal arms.

DEVOTIONAL STATUES

Many Christians, Roman Catholics especially, use statues as aids to prayer. Statues of Mary, the mother of Jesus, are a common feature of Roman Catholic churches. Many Roman Catholics pray that Mary will intercede on their behalf, placing votive candles in front of her image. In Roman Catholic countries, statues and banners are often carried in procession through the streets during religious festivals.

ICONS

Icons are stylised religious pictures, usually painted on blocks of wood, that are used mainly by Orthodox Christians (see page 25). They are believed to provide a window into the spiritual world. Icons can be large, such as those painted on the walls of Orthodox churches, or small and portable. Orthodox Christians will have a personal icon of their own patron saint, and many will also have icons of Jesus, Mary, John the Baptist and other saints. Many miracles are attributed to icons and they are objects of great devotion. Candles are lit in front of them and prayers are said before them. During festivals, icons are carried in procession.

The design of icons adheres to strict conventions. The perspective used in icons is often reversed so that the worshipper is drawn into an ever-expanding world, rather than one which recedes towards a vanishing point. The eyes of the people depicted in icons always stare straight out at the viewer. One worshipper has said that to look into these unblinking but deeply compassionate eyes is to feel that the innermost reaches of one's soul are being examined, but that in those eyes one can glimpse eternity.

PATEN AND CHALICE (see page 26)

In many Churches (including the Church of England and the Roman Catholic Church), the Communion bread (usually in the form of wafers) is placed on a small plate called a paten and the wine is poured into a goblet called a chalice. The paten and chalice are usually made of precious metal and adorned with jewels, but they can be of more humble design, made of wood or pottery.

INCENSE

Incense is a spice which is burned over charcoal in a container called a censer or a thurible, usually made of silver. In Roman Catholic, Orthodox and 'High' Anglican church services, the censer or thurible is swung from a chain, allowing sweet smelling smoke to fill the air. For many Christians, this helps to create an atmosphere that aids prayer.

BAPTISM (see page 22)

Baptismal Candle

In some churches, during the baptism service, a small candle may be lit from the Paschal candle (see below) and given to the parents or godparents on behalf of the child with words such as the following: *'Receive this light. This is to show you have passed from darkness into light. Shine as the light of the world'.* The candle is often kept as a memento.

Baptismal Certificate

The Certificate of Baptism records the place and date of baptism and the promises made by the Godparents on the child's behalf.

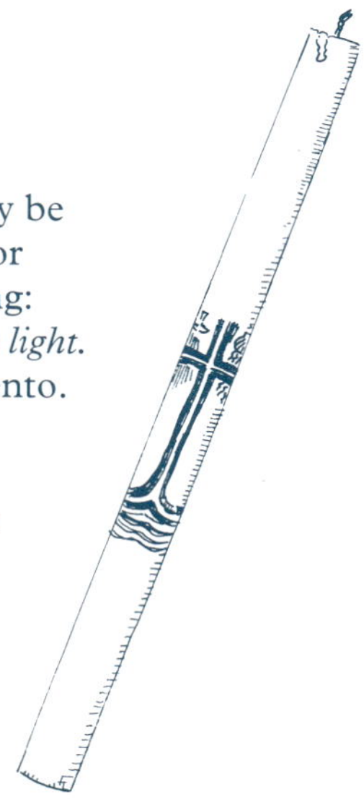

ADVENT (see page 19)

Advent Candle

Advent candles are occasionally found in churches. The candle is divided into 24 numbered sections. Every day from 1 December until Christmas, a section of the candle is burnt down.

Advent Calendar

Each day from 1 December, a window or door (numbered from 1 to 25) is opened to display a picture associated with Christmas.

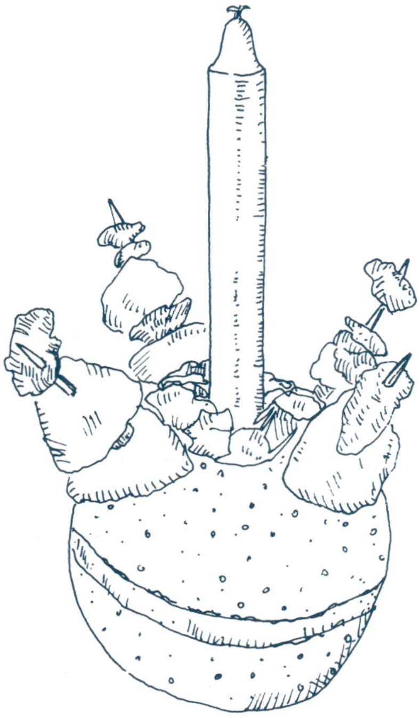

Advent Wreath

An Advent wreath usually comprises a circle of evergreen leaves, such as holly, with four small red or purple candles placed around it and a large white candle in the middle. One of the outer candles is lit on the first Sunday in Advent, two on the second and so on, until Christmas Day, when all the candles are lit, including the large central one. This celebrates the birth of Jesus, the light of the world.

Christingle

Christingle services are held in many churches during the week before Christmas. A Christingle is an orange, with a red ribbon around the centre, into which four cocktail sticks are pushed. Soft fruits and sweets are impaled on the cocktail sticks. A candle is inserted into the top of the orange, and lit.

The orange represents the world.
The red ribbon represents the blood which Jesus shed.
The four cocktail sticks represent the four seasons.
The fruit and the sweets represent the fruits of the earth.
The candle represents Jesus, the light of the world.

HOLY WEEK

Palm Cross

Small crosses made from palm leaves are distributed in churches on Palm Sunday (see page 20). These may be burnt the following year to make ash for the Ash Wednesday service (see page 20).

Paschal Candle

The Paschal candle is a large candle traditionally lit at the evening service on Holy Saturday (see page 21). After the Easter season it is usually placed near the font and used in baptisms.

LITURGICAL COLOURS

Roman Catholic practice is generally followed in Anglican churches where colour is accepted as an aid to worship. The colours worn by the priest on some of the more important days of the Church year are as follows:

Ordinary Sundays and weekdays: *green.*
Advent and Lent: *violet (or blue).*
Christmas, Epiphany, Maundy Thursday, Easter Day Trinity Sunday and for saints: *white (or gold).*
Palm Sunday, Pentecost and feasts of Apostles and Martyrs: *red.*
All Souls' Day: *violet (or black).*

Above: *Church of England vestments.*

1 Chasuble
2 Maniple
3 Girdle
4 Stole
5 Alb
6 Surplice
7 Tippet
8 Cassock
9 Hood

SYMBOLS

THE CROSS

The cross is the universal symbol of Christianity. It serves as a reminder of the suffering that Jesus endured for humanity when he was crucified, and the empty cross recalls the resurrection.

THE CHI RO

The Chi Ro is a monogram of the first two letters, Chi (X) and Rho (P), of the Greek word for Christ.

THE IHS

I, H and S are the first three letters (iota, eta and sigma) of the Greek spelling of Jesus.

THE ALPHA AND OMEGA

Alpha is the first letter of the Greek alphabet and Omega is the last. God and Jesus are at the beginning and end of all things.

THE FISH

The initial letters of the Greek words for 'Jesus Christ, God's Son, Saviour' (Iesous CHristos THeou Uios Soter), spell the Greek word for fish (ICHTHUS). The fish was a secret sign used by members of the early Church in Rome when they were being persecuted. It is also a reminder that many of Jesus' disciples were fishermen.

THE DOVE

The dove is a well-known symbol of peace, but in a specifically Christian context it symbolises the Holy Spirit. At Jesus' baptism, the Holy Spirit came down 'like a dove'. In the story of Noah, a dove was sent out from the ark three times. The first time it returned without anything. The second time it returned with an olive leaf. The third time, having found dry land, it did not return.

Hinduism

ALL THIS UNIVERSE IS IN TRUTH BRAHMAN.
He is the beginning and end and life of all.
As such, in silence, give unto him adoration...
There is a spirit that is mind and life,
light and truth and vast spaces.
He contains all works and desires
and all perfumes and all tastes.
He enfolds the whole universe,
and in silence is loving to all...
This is the Spirit that is in my heart,
this is Brahman.
To him I shall come when I go beyond this life.
And to him will come he who has faith and doubts not.

From the Chandogya Upanishad 3

Hinduism

BACKGROUND INFORMATION

INDIA

Hinduism is closely linked with India, a land of many languages and cultures, of modern cities and traditional villages. Bounded to the north by the Himalayan mountains and on the other two sides of its triangular shape by oceans, India is largely a vast fertile plain. The mountains, and the rivers which flow from them, play a significant part in the spiritual life of the people of India. Most sacred of all is the River Ganges, which flows through the holy city of Varanasi (formerly known as Banaras).

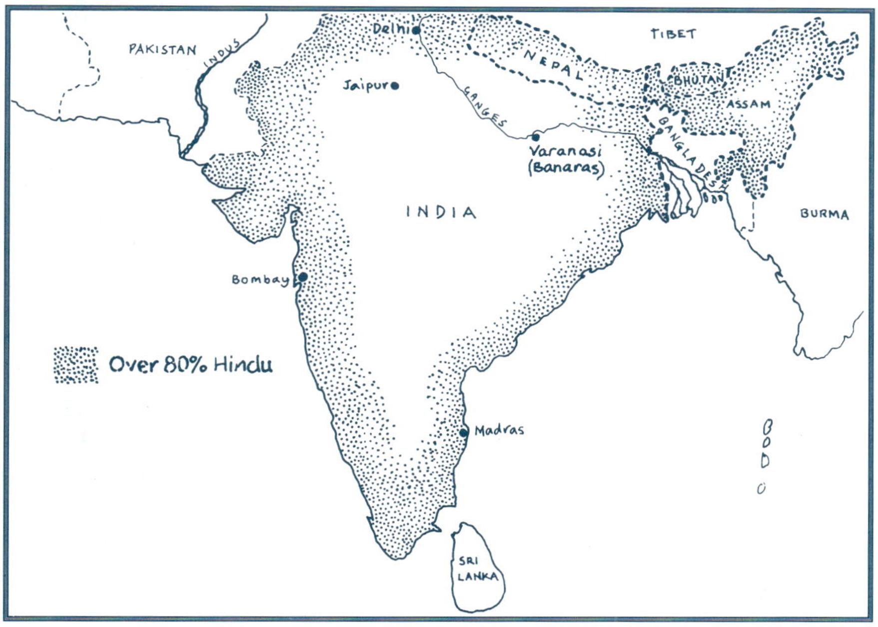

HINDUS TODAY

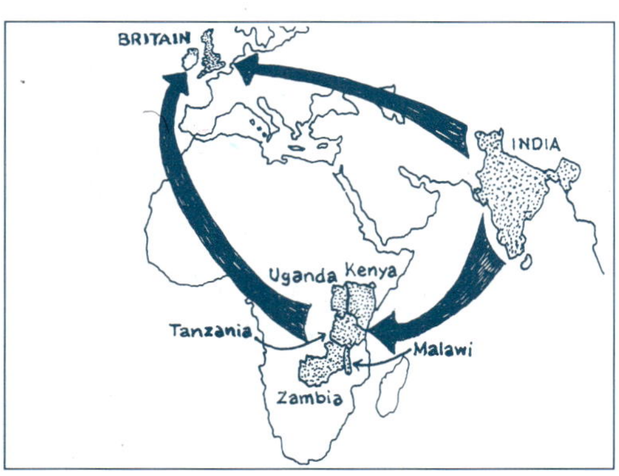

The global population of Hindus has been estimated at 500 million, the great majority of whom live in India. There are over 400,000 Hindus in Britain. The families of many Hindus came to Britain from African countries such as Kenya, Tanzania, Uganda, Zambia and Malawi.

ORIGINS

The terms Hindu and Hinduism are widely used, but it is important to note that they do not appear in any Indian scriptural writings. Hinduism is a recently invented and misleading term introduced by people from outside the tradition. Use of this term gives the impression of a coherent, unified and institutionalised religion, rather than a diverse tradition characterised by a wide range of beliefs and practices. Followers of the tradition prefer the phrase Sanatan Dharma (*the Eternal* or *Imperishable Religion*), but purely for convenience the term Hinduism is used in this publication.

Hinduism is not based on any one person's life and teachings. There is no acknowledged founder of Hinduism. The roots of the religion can be traced back to between 1700 and 1500 BCE, when light-skinned Aryan invaders destroyed the civilisation that then existed in northwest India, before taking over central and southern India.

Archaeological excavations at Mohenjodaro and Harappa in the Indus Valley have revealed that the pre-Aryan civilisation in northwest India was sophisticated and well-ordered. It seems likely that the religious tradition known as Hinduism emerged through the interaction of the beliefs and practices of the Aryan invaders with those of the earlier inhabitants of the Indus Valley.

***Above:** Priest-king or deity from Mohenjodaro, 2000-1750 BCE.*

BELIEFS AND WAY OF LIFE

(For descriptions of some of the principal Hindu deities, see page 47 ff)

BRAHMAN AND ATMAN

Most Hindus follow the Vedanta tradition, which is a system of beliefs derived from ancient religious writings called the Vedas. Within the Vedanta system there are two main schools of thought, the Advaita and the Dvaita.

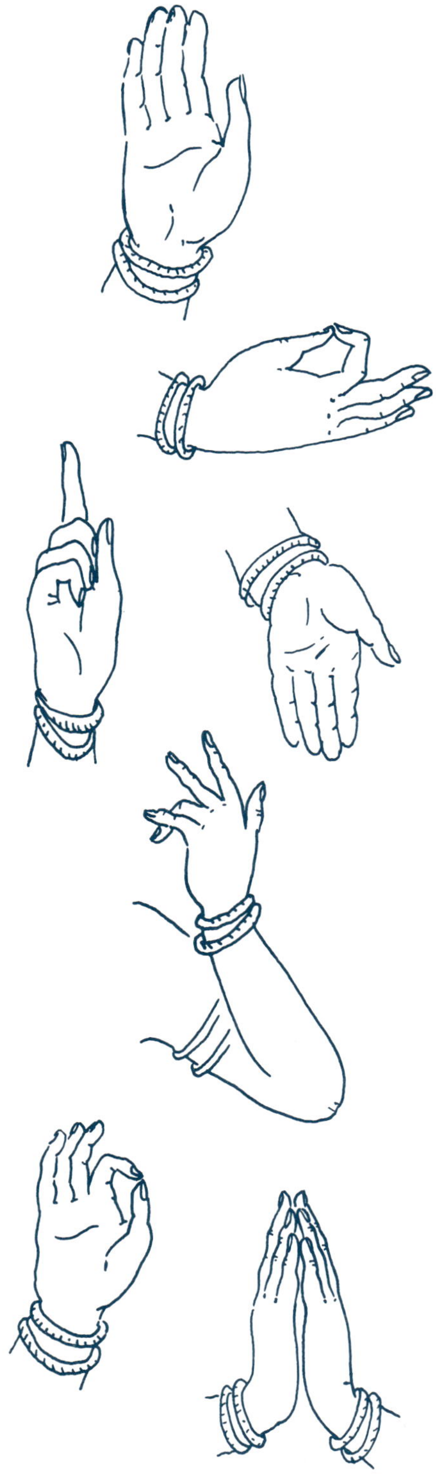

The 'language of gestures of the gods' (mudras).
From top: *Abhaya (blessing, protection and reassurance); Jnana (wisdom as a quality of the god concerned); Tarjani (threat or warning); Varada (the god is preparing to grant a wish or bestow a blessing); Vismaya (surprise or wonder recognising the superiority of another god present); Vitarka (god is proving pure judgement and intellectual wisdom); Anjali (in front of the chest–worship), Namaskara (in front of the forehead–greeting).*

The Advaita tradition perceives Brahman (the universal cosmic soul) as the ultimate reality: that from which everything emanates, in which everything resides and into which everything is ultimately dissolved. Brahman has no personal name or gender and is seen more in terms of all-pervading energy than of personality. In the Advaita view, the aim of life is seen as the merging of Atman (the individual soul) with Brahman. When this fusion happens, a person is released from the round of life, death and rebirth and achieves Moksha (ultimate liberation).

Those who adhere to the Dvaita tradition are monotheists who believe that God has a personality in some ways resembling that of human beings. However, they believe that Atman is essentially distinct from God and that liberation is found in eternal service to the Godhead.

ONE AND MANY

Hindus believe in one central Godhead which is manifested in many different ways. There are many thousands of gods and goddesses, each of which embodies a different aspect of the Divine:

'That which is One, the wise call by many names.' (Rig Veda)

The energy associated with Brahman is manifested in the Trimurti (*the three deities*):

> ***Brahma*** is the manifestation of the force or energy that creates and brings things into being.
> ***Vishnu*** is the manifestation of the force or energy that sustains the created order.
> ***Shiva*** is the manifestation of the force or energy that destroys everything.

The Pama Purana describes how Brahman wished to create the world. To do this, he created himself from his own left side in the form of Brahma. In order to maintain what he had created, he brought forth Vishnu from his right side, and in order to be able to destroy everything, he created Shiva from the centre of his body.

THE AVATARS OF VISHNU

Avatar means 'one who descends'. Vishnu is believed to have appeared on earth many times taking on different forms, some human and some animal. Most Hindus accept that there are ten Avatars (incarnations) of Vishnu: Matsya (the fish-man), Kurma (the tortoise-man), Varaha (the boar-man), Narasimha (the lion-man), Vamana (the dwarf), Parashurama (Rama with an axe), Rama, Krishna, the Buddha and Kalki (the appearance of Vishnu on a white horse at the end of the present age). Of these, the most significant for Hindus are Rama and Krishna.

Rama, whose story is told in the Ramayana (see page 37), is regarded as the perfect model of manhood.

Krishna is worshipped with particular devotion. He appears as Arjuna's charioteer in the Bhagavad Gita (see page 37), and many stories are told about him as a baby, a child and a young man. His mischievous pranks include stealing cream and playing tricks on the Gopis (the cowherds' daughters).

THE TRIMURTI, AND SOME ASSOCIATED DEITIES

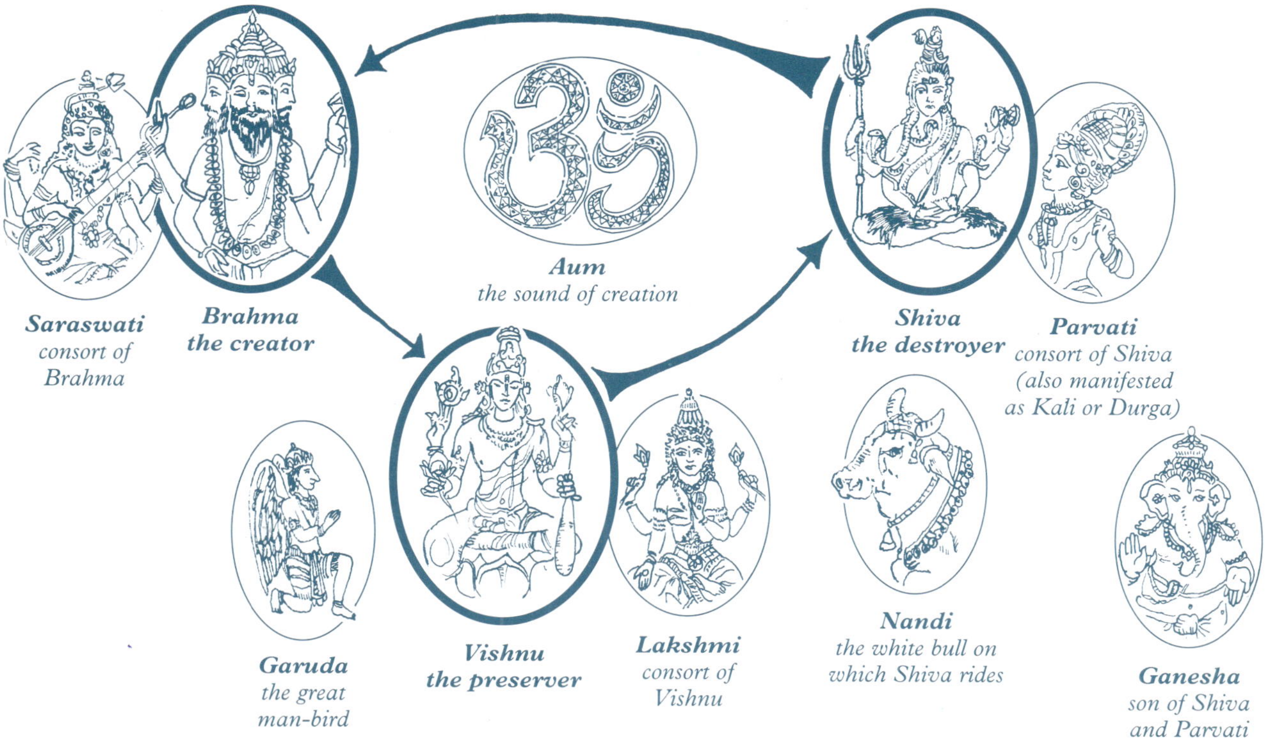

THE TEN AVATARS OF VISHNU, AND SOME ASSOCIATED DEITIES

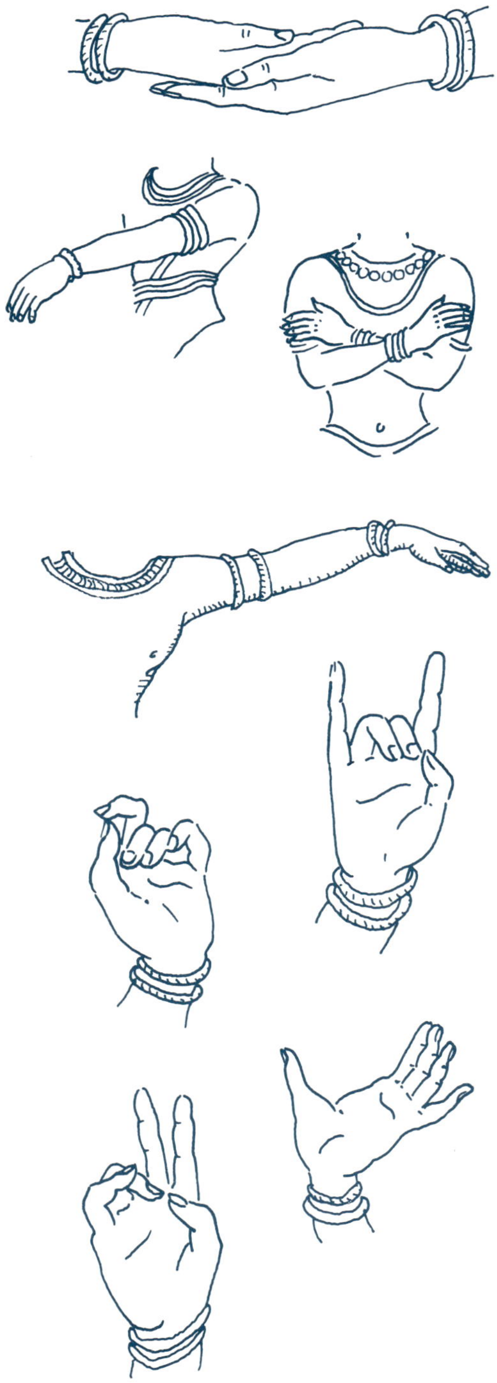

The 'language of gestures of the gods' (mudras).
From top: *Dhyana (meditation); Gaja (symbol of elephant's trunk–great strength and power, Shiva-Nataraja); Hastasvastika (total surrender to a god in a superior position); Pataka (wing of a bird–strength, or refers to the power of flames of a fire); Damaru (holding a drum); Kataka (holding a lotus flower); Ardhacandra (carrying fire); Kartari (symbolises the antlers of a deer, representing the contradictions inherent in all things).*

Vishnu's consort, Lakshmi, is associated with wealth and good fortune. She sometimes takes on human form, appearing as Sita, Rama's wife. She also appears as Radha, the consort of Krishna.

SHIVA AND PARVATI

Shiva embodies destructive energy, but in the action of destroying, he paves the way for renewal and re-creation. He is often associated with fertility.

Shiva's consort is Parvati, who also appears as the goddesses Durga and Kali. Like Shiva, Durga and Kali, the Black One, are associated with death and destruction.

Shakti is the energy or power associated with Hindu gods and goddesses generally, but Shakti also refers specifically to the female energy or power of Shiva, which is manifested in Parvati, Durga and Kali.

NATURE GODS AND ANIMAL GODS

The early Hindu gods (the gods of the Aryan invaders) were manifestations of elemental natural forces. These included Agni (the god of fire), Surya (the sun god) and Indra (the most powerful of all ancient gods: the god of thunder and lightning).

Hindus treat all life-forms as sacred and animals play an important part in Hindu mythology. One of the most popular gods is Ganesha, the son of Shiva and Parvati. Ganesha has an elephant's head, and he is regarded as the remover of obstacles and the bringer of good fortune. The first prayers in Puja (*worship*) are always offered to Ganesha.

Shiva rides a white bull called Nandi and Vishnu rides the great man-bird Garuda. Hanuman, the monkey god, is the faithful friend and helper of Rama and Sita.

REINCARNATION

A fundamental belief shared by all Hindus is that each soul is reincarnated many times on this earth. As one body grows old and dies, the soul enters a new body:

'As a person puts on new garments, giving up the old ones, the soul similarly accepts new material bodies, giving up the old, the useless ones.'
(Bhagavad Gita)

SAMSARA AND KARMA

The soul's passage through a series of lives in different species (human, animal, etc) is called Samsara. The body that the soul enters is determined by Karma: the law of cause and effect. Good actions in one life ensure that the soul will enter a body with a higher quality of existence in the next. Bad actions will result in a poorer quality of rebirth.

FOUR PATHS TO LIBERATION

Moksha (liberation from the cycle of life, death and rebirth) can be achieved in four main ways:

> ***Bhakti-yoga*** (the path of devotion to God)
> ***Karma-yoga*** (the path of good works)
> ***Jnana-yoga*** (the path of knowledge)
> ***Yoga*** (spiritual practices such as meditation)

VARNAS

Hindu society traditionally divides people into four main Varnas (*divisions*). The role that a person plays in society is determined by the Varna into which that person is born:

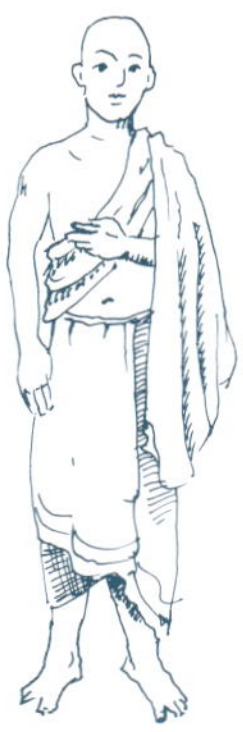

Brahmins are priests and teachers

Kshatriyas are rulers, administrators and military leaders

Vaishyas are merchants and farmers

Shudras are artisans and manual labourers

Each of these groups is further sub-divided into various castes.

Falling outside this system are Pariahs, those who traditionally perform the most degrading tasks. These people are often referred to as Outcastes or Untouchables, but to Mahatma Gandhi they were Harijans (*Children of God*).

Many Hindus have now chosen to reject strict adherence to the caste system.

ASHRAMAS

Hindus see life as having four Ashramas (*stages*). Males belonging to the first three Varnas are traditionally expected to live out these stages. The four Ashramas are as follows:

As a Brahmacharaya (*student*) one lives as an ascetic and is taught by a Guru.

As a Grihastha (*householder*) one marries and brings up children.

As a Vanaprastha (*'retirer'*) one begins to withdraw from society to concentrate on spiritual matters.

As a Sannyasin (*'renouncer'*) one gives up all worldly affairs and attachments and lives as a wandering ascetic.

Above: *Having left the householder stage, an elderly man reads in a peaceful location.*

DHARMA

Dharma is a central concept in Hinduism, but it is difficult to convey all that it means in English. One aspect of Dharma is religious duty. Each person has a duty to contribute to society and this duty is determined by factors such as family background, caste and stage of life.

Dharma also refers to what might be termed the essence or intrinsic quality of something. Thus the Dharma of water is wetness. The Dharma of all living beings is seen as service to the Divine.

Above: *The cow is most sacred of all animals; 'The Breath of Life takes living creatures as its garments'.* (Atharva Veda XI)

AHIMSA

Hindus believe in the equality of all living beings and in the sanctity of life. The concept of Ahimsa embraces the idea of respect for all life forms and of non-violence. In India the cow (upon which so much of the traditional way of life has depended) is treated as the most sacred of all animals. Most Hindus are vegetarians.

PUJA IN THE HOME

In most Hindu homes there is a shrine containing statues and pictures of various gods and goddesses. Every day, often in the morning after bathing, the family performs Puja (*worship*). Puja involves the five senses

Centre: *A typical shrine in the home.*

and makes symbolic reference to the four elements (earth, air, fire and water). The fruits of the earth (rice, nuts, fruit, flowers, etc) are offered to the images of the deities. Incense is burned and lamps are lit. Water is used to wash the divine images. Bells are rung and finger cymbals are chimed. Prayers, including the Gayatri mantra, are sung and chanted.

The Gayatri Mantra:
Aum.
O terrestrial sphere.
O sphere of space.
O celestial sphere.
Let us contemplate the splendour of the Spirit,
the divine creator.
May he guide our minds
and inspire us with understanding.

WRITINGS

THE FOUR VEDAS

The Vedas were composed in Sanskrit between 1700 and 1500 BCE by Aryan invaders of India. The most important of the Vedas is the Rig Veda, a collection of about a thousand hymns of praise to gods such as Agni, Surya and Indra. Many of the hymns of the Rig Veda are also found in the Sama Veda. The Yajur Veda deals with sacrificial ritual, and the Atharva Veda contains spells and incantations.

THE UPANISHADS

Upanishad literally means 'sit down near'. The Upanishads are a collection of religious and philosophical writings exploring the relationship between Atman and Brahman. They were written in Sanskrit between 600 and 200 BCE.

THE MAHABHARATA

This epic poem (probably the world's longest) was originally composed in about the 9th century BCE. It tells of a long-lasting war between two families, the Pandavas and the Kauravas.

The Bhagavad Gita

The most famous part of the Mahabharata is the Bhagavad Gita (*the Song of the Lord*). Most Hindus regard this as their most important scripture.

The Bhagavad Gita is set on a battlefield. The army of the Pandavas and the army of the Kauravas are lined up against each other. In the lull before the fighting, Arjuna (one of the five Pandava brothers) rides up and down between the two armies in his chariot. He knows that many of his relatives are in the opposing army, and when he contemplates the carnage that is about to take place, he is overwhelmed with sadness and despair. He realises that he cannot fight and orders his charioteer to withdraw.

The charioteer is really Krishna, and instead of complying with Arjuna's wishes, he starts a philosophical debate. The subsequent dialogue epitomises much that is contained in contemporary Hindu thought.

Krishna's teaching as presented in the Bhagavad Gita is mainly concerned with Bhakti (*devotion* or *love*). The central message is that the highest form of worship is devotion to God. Any action is acceptable so long as it is carried out as an expression of Bhakti. Arjuna is a warrior and his Dharma (*duty*) is to fight. If he fights selflessly in a spirit of love and devotion to God, he will have performed Bhakti.

So, with Krishna at his side, Arjuna enters the battle and helps to defeat the Kaurava army.

THE RAMAYANA

The Ramayana epic is much shorter than the Mahabharata (about a tenth of its length). It was first written down in Sanskrit between 200 BCE and 200 CE. According to tradition it is the work of one man, the sage Valmiki.

SHRUTI AND SMRITI

The sacred writings of Hinduism are divided into two groups:
Shruti (*that which is heard*) and
Smriti (*that which is remembered*).

Shruti comprises the four Vedas and the Upanishads. Smriti includes the Mahabharata (containing the Bhagavad Gita), the Ramayana, the Laws of Manu and the Puranas.

Above: *Arjuna in his chariot. The charioteer is Krishna.*

Above: *The Ramayana in comic form.*

The Ramayana tells the story of Rama and Sita: the ideal man and the ideal woman united in ideal love. The end of the story (re-lived at the festival of Divali) celebrates the triumph of good over evil and the beginning of Rama's rule: a golden age of peace and prosperity, justice and happiness.

The story is very popular in India and beyond. As well as being told, it is acted out, danced and performed by puppets.

The story tells of how Prince Rama came to hear of a beautiful princess called Sita. Many men wanted to marry her, but her father had vowed that she would marry the first man to string an enormous bow that he possessed. Many had tried, but until Rama's arrival no one had managed even to lift it up. Rama picked up the bow as though it weighed nothing. When he drew back the bow-string, the great bow snapped in half. So, at a magnificent wedding ceremony, Sita became Rama's wife.

Rama's father, King Dasharatha, was old, and Rama's stepmother was going to make absolutely certain that when he died, Rama would not replace him as king. She reminded her ailing husband that many years before he had promised her anything she wanted. Now she demanded that her son Bharata become King Dasharatha's heir, and that Rama be banished to the forest for fourteen years. Sita and Lakshman, Rama's brother, went with Rama into the forest, and Bharata became king. But by placing Rama's shoes on the throne, he showed that he was king only until Rama's return.

One day, Sita saw a beautiful deer running through the forest. Its golden coat was studded with jewels. She asked Rama to catch it for her. Leaving Sita under Lakshman's protection, Rama gave chase. Rama was gone for a long time, and Sita grew anxious. Eventually she persuaded Lakshman to leave her and to go and find Rama. What none of them realised was that the deer was really an evil demon in disguise that had been sent by Ravana to lure Rama and Lakshman away from Sita. Ravana was a dreadful demon-king with ten heads. He seized the unprotected Sita and imprisoned her on his island kingdom of Lanka.

Rama and Lakshman eventually found out where Ravana was holding Sita, and with the help of Hanuman, the monkey-king, and his monkey army, they built a bridge from the mainland to the island of Lanka. After many weeks of fighting, during the last terrible battle, Rama faced Ravana alone. Rama drew back his bow and shot a special arrow at Ravana. This was Indra's dart, with a tip made from sunlight and fire. The arrow pierced Ravana's heart and the demon lay dead. Rama and Sita were re-united, and eventually they returned to their kingdom. Bharata welcomed his brother as the rightful king and everyone celebrated. Thousands of Divas (*small clay lamps*) were lit to welcome them home, an event recalled during the festival of Divali (see page 39).

THE LAWS OF MANU

The Laws of Manu were written at about the same time as the Bhagavad Gita. They are rules governing everyday life, with appropriate punishments prescribed for wrong-doers.

THE PURANAS

These are comparatively recent collections of stories, only about a thousand years old. Many of the stories are about gods and goddesses, including the tales of Krishna's childhood.

THE PANCHATANTRA AND THE HITOPADESH

The Panchatantra (*Five Books*) is an anonymous collection of ancient tales and moral fables.

Above: *Krishna saving the cows and his friends by inhaling the flames of a forest fire.*

Twenty-five of the fables contained in the Panchatantra are also included, along with seventeen other stories, in a later collection of moral fables called the Hitopadesh (*Friendly Advice* or *Salutary Instruction*).

Many of the Panchatantra stories and all of the tales in the Hitopadesh feature animals with human or superhuman qualities. They are similar to Aesop's fables.

FESTIVALS

In addition to the main Hindu festivals, there are many local festivities. There are regional variations with regard to the timing of festivals and the way that they are celebrated. Some of the more important festivals are described below.

DIVALI (October/November)

Divali is the Hindu New Year festival, lasting between two and five days. It is the most widely celebrated of all Indian festivals (it is celebrated by Sikhs as well as Hindus), and the celebrations take on a variety of local forms. In the days leading up to Divali, homes and business premises are cleaned and redecorated. During the festival, gifts and cards are exchanged.

Divali means 'row of lights'. During the festival, Divas (small clay lamps–see page 51) are put along window ledges and on the roofs of houses. The lights serve a two-fold purpose. They recall the story of the return from exile of Rama and Sita, when people lit lamps to celebrate their return to their kingdom (see page 38). They are also lit to welcome the goddess Lakshmi into the home. Elaborate Rangoli patterns made from coloured sand, chalks and flour, are painstakingly created on floors. These also serve to attract Lakshmi into the home.

Above: *Divali card featuring the goddess Lakshmi.*

Above: *Saraswati.*

Lakshmi (see page 48) is the goddess of wealth, prosperity and happiness. Lakshmi Puja (worship of Lakshmi) is a central feature of Divali. Business people close their accounts before participating in Lakshmi Puja.

VASANTA PANCHAMI / SARASWATI PUJA (January/February)

Vasanta Panchami marks the beginning of spring. In some places the festival is known as Saraswati Puja, and it is dedicated to Saraswati (see page 47), the goddess of learning and the arts. In west Bengal, clay images of Saraswati are carried in procession before being immersed in rivers or ponds.

HOLI (February/March)

Holi is a north Indian spring festival. The celebrations recall the mischievous pranks of Krishna (see page 32). People throw coloured water and powder over each other and play practical jokes.

During the festival, Hindus also remember how Vishnu rescued his devotee Prahlada from the evil Holika (see story below). Holika tried to burn Prahlada to death on a bonfire, and on the eve of Holi huge bonfires are lit. The name Holi comes from Holika.

The story behind Holi

There was a king called Hiranyakashup who had a son called Prahlada. Prahlada was brought up believing that his father was a god. One day Prahlada heard a potter praying to the god Vishnu, and later he learned that the potter's prayer had been answered. From that day on, Prahlada refused to pray to his father.

His father became very angry and punished his son, but Prahlada still refused to believe that his father was a god. The king decided he must kill his son. He told his soldiers to dig a deep pit and to fill it with poisonous snakes. Prahlada was thrown into the pit. Many snakes bit him, but Vishnu protected him and he did not die.

The king then sent a herd of elephants to trample on Prahlada while he slept, but again Vishnu protected him and he remained unharmed.

The king refused to give up and sent his soldiers with swords to kill Prahlada. Although he was stabbed many times, Prahlada again remained unhurt.

Finally the king requested help from his evil sister Holika. She said she would take Prahlada into the midst of a huge bonfire and hold on to him until he burned to death. She would protect herself from the flames by magic. Holika pulled Prahlada into the great bonfire and held tightly on to him while the flames raged around them. When the bonfire died down, with Vishnu's protection, Prahlada emerged alive and unharmed. It was Holika who had been burned to death.

RAMNAVAMI (March/April)

Ramnavami celebrates the birth of Rama, hero of the Ramayana (see page 38). Rama's birth is re-enacted in many Mandirs (*temples*). Images or pictures of the infant Rama are placed in cradles which are uncovered at midday. Worshippers take turns in rocking the cradle.

RATHA-YATRA / JAGANNATHA (June/July)

A characteristic feature of many Hindu festivals is the procession of images of various deities through the streets. The images are often carried on large wheeled vehicles. Such a procession is called a Ratha-Yatra (*chariot journey*).

The most spectacular Ratha-Yatra takes place in the city of Puri in Orissa. Every year, the image of Krishna (see page 48) is brought out of the Mandir (*temple*) to be bathed, anointed, cleaned and repainted. It is then placed on a huge wooden cart (about 15 metres high) and towed by hundreds, or even thousands, of people to another Mandir in the city. The same thing happens to images of Subhadra, Krishna's sister, and Balarama, his brother. After a few days, the three images are pulled back to their original shrines. The English word 'juggernaut' comes from the name by which Krishna is known during this festival: Jagannatha.

RAKSHA BANDHAN (July/August)

Raksha Bandhan is a family festival, during which sisters thank their brothers for the love they have shown by tying Rakhis (decorated bracelets made of silk or cotton–see pages 51) around their brothers' wrists. In return, brothers give their sisters presents or money. Rakhis are also said to ward off evil. Raksha means 'protection' and Bandhan means 'to tie'.

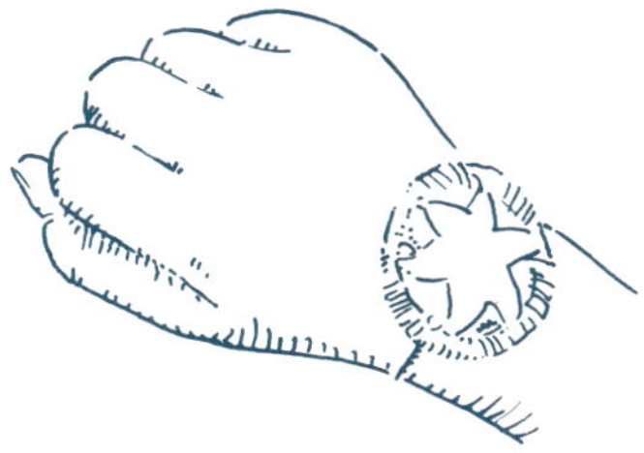

Above: *A rakhi bracelet.*

JANMASHTAMI (August/September)

Janmashtami celebrates the birth of Krishna (see story below and pages 32 and 48). Many Hindus fast until midnight, when Krishna is said to have been born. The baby god is then greeted with singing and dancing and food offerings. In Hindu homes and temples, images of the baby Krishna are placed on small swings or in cradles.

The story behind Janmashtami

The demon-king Kamsa was evil and cruel. When one of his advisers prophesied that his sister, Devaki, would give birth to a child that would kill him, he imprisoned her together with her husband, Vasudeva. The couple had six children in prison. As each baby was born, the child was taken away and killed.

The god Vishnu decided to intervene. Devaki became pregnant and gave birth to a baby boy called Krishna (really Vishnu). Krishna was born at midnight, and as soon as he was born he stood up and spoke to Vasudeva, his father. The baby Krishna told Vasudeva to exchange him with a baby girl who had been born to the wife of a cowherd called Nanda. Nanda's dwelling was on the far side of the river Yamuna.

No sooner had Krishna spoken than the chains that were holding his father broke, the guards fell into a deep sleep, and the doors of the prison swung open. Carrying his child in a basket, Vasudeva ran until he stood on the banks of the Yamuna. Now his heart sank, for the great

river was in flood. However, as soon as he stepped into the raging torrent, the waters parted and he was able to cross safely to the other side. He wasted no time in finding Nanda's house, where he secretly exchanged Krishna for the cowherd's daughter. Vasudeva returned safely to the prison (the waters of the Yamuna again divided to allow him to pass), and there he placed the baby girl in Krishna's cradle. The prison doors slammed shut and the broken chains became whole again. The baby's cries roused the guards, who hurried to tell Kamsa that his sister had given birth to another child.

As soon as Kamsa heard the news, he rushed to the prison with a drawn sword in his hand. As the evil demon-king approached the baby with his sword raised ready to kill her, she stood up in her cot and told him that she was really the goddess Yogamaya and that Krishna was alive and well. One day the prophecy would come true, and Krishna would kill the evil king.

GANESHA-CHATURTHI (August/September)

Ganesha-Chaturthi celebrates the birth of Ganesha (see story below and page 50). Ganesha is the popular elephant-headed god of good fortune and the remover of obstacles. In many places in India, clay images of Ganesha (some of them very large) are worshipped and paraded noisily through the streets before being immersed in tanks of water or the sea.

The story behind Ganesha-Chaturthi

The god Shiva and his wife Parvati were very happy. There was just one thing that marred their joy: they had no children.

One day, while Parvati was bathing, she took some soap and moulded it, with a few flakes of her skin, into a human shape. When she breathed on the tiny figure, it came to life. The figure grew into a handsome boy, whom she named Ganesha.

Ganesha stood guard whenever his mother bathed. On one occasion, Shiva had been away from Parvati for so long that when he returned, he did not recognise the boy who stood barring his way. When Ganesha refused to let him enter his own home, Shiva lost his temper and in the heat of the moment he struck off the boy's head.

Parvati was heartbroken, and so Shiva promised to make amends. He sent his servants to find the head of another child, but every child they found was gazing at its mother and they did not have the heart to separate them. Eventually they found a baby elephant, sleeping with its head away from its mother so that their trunks did not get entwined.

They brought the baby elephant's head back to Shiva, who placed it on Ganesha's shoulders and restored the boy to life. Parvati soon grew to love her elephant-headed son, who is one of the most popular of all Hindu deities.

NAVARATRI / DURGA PUJA / DASSEHRA / VIJAY DASHAMI

(September/October)

This nine or ten-day festival (Navaratri means 'nine nights' and Dassehra means 'ten days') is celebrated throughout India in a wide variety of ways. During the festival, Hindus remember how the goddess Durga defeated Mahishasura, the evil buffalo-demon (see story on page 43). Images of Durga (see page 50) sitting astride her lion are worshipped for nine days, and on the tenth day (Dassehra) they are immersed in water.

In parts of north India, the celebrations recall the story of Rama and Sita (see page 38). The Ramayana is acted out in plays called Ram Lila.

In Delhi there is an impressive Ram Lila which lasts throughout the ten days of the festival. On the tenth day (Dassehra) there is a spectacular finale. The actor playing Rama fires a burning arrow into a huge effigy of the demon Ravana, which bursts into flames sending fireworks shooting in all directions.

In the state of Gujurat an important feature of the celebrations is the Dandia Ras (*stick dance*). Many Hindu communities in Britain have taken up this tradition.

The story behind Durga Puja

Mahishasura, the evil buffalo-demon, was threatening to destroy the earth and all the gods. None of the gods could defeat him. They decided to send the goddess Durga against him, armed with an array of weapons including Shiva's trident, Vishnu's disc, Agni's dart, Surya's arrows and Indra's thunderbolt.

Riding on a ferocious lion, Durga led her army against Mahishasura's forces. When it became apparent that her army was succeeding in overcoming the troops of Mahishasura, the buffalo-demon flew into a terrible rage. The earth shook and the waters foamed. He thundered towards Durga, lashing out with his horns, his hooves and his tail and killing many of her followers.

Durga succeeded in lassoing him, but he turned into a lion and escaped. Durga gave chase and cut off the lion's head, but he turned into a man. Durga shot the man with arrows, but he turned into an elephant. Durga cut off the elephant's trunk, but he turned back into a buffalo. Durga leapt onto the buffalo's neck and plunged Shiva's trident into him. At last he lay dead.

All of Creation rejoiced except for the forces of evil, which ran away in confusion.

RITES OF PASSAGE

BIRTH

The First Nine Samskars

There are sixteen traditional stages in the Hindu life cycle, each of them marked by a ritual called a Samskar. Nine of the Samskars are associated with birth, but they are not practised by all Hindus. The first nine are as follows:

1 The intending parents ask the priest to identify the most auspicious occasion for sexual intercourse.

2 The mother recites passages from the scriptures to the baby in her womb.

3 So as not to harm the baby, the mother avoids foods that are salty or spicy.

4 After birth, the baby is washed and the sacred syllable ***Aum*** is written in honey on the baby's tongue with a golden pen.

5 There is a naming ceremony, during which Prashad (a mixture of dried fruits, nuts and sugar crystals) is eaten. Syllables that are suitable for the child's name are suggested by the priest, based on the baby's horoscope.

Above: *Horoscopes are often consulted in India.*

6 The baby goes on her/his first outing.	**7** The child is given rice pudding by the maternal uncle made at a ceremony in the home.
8 The child's ears are pierced.	**9** The child's head is shaved to remove any misfortune carried over from the previous life.

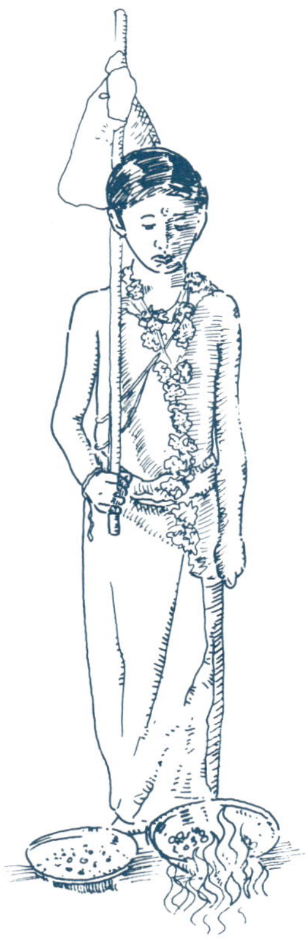

Above: *A boy at the Sacred Thread Ceremony.*
Below: *A Hindu bride.*

COMING OF AGE

The 'sacred thread' ceremony
The 'sacred thread' ceremony is not practised by all Hindus, but some boys belonging to the three upper Varnas (social divisions–see page 35) are presented with a sacred thread. When a boy is between eight and twelve years old, he goes through a symbolic second birth. His head is shaved and a circle made of cotton thread with three strands is placed over his shoulder and across his body. The strands are tied together with a knot called a Brahma Granthi (*spiritual knot*). The thread must be worn at all times. The boy takes vows accepting the duties of manhood and is given presents. The family then celebrates with a meal.

MARRIAGE

Hindu weddings are symbolic of the alliance of two families, so it is the parents who usually choose their child's partner. Horoscopes are consulted to confirm the compatibility of the couple and to set the wedding day. In India, weddings usually take place in the bride's family home or in the Mandir (*temple*). In Britain, a community centre or a hired hall is generally used. To ensure that they are blessed with good fortune, both bride and groom worship Ganesha (the elephant-headed god–see page 50) on the day before the wedding.

The bride spends a long time getting ready for the wedding, assisted by female members of her family and friends. She wears a red sari decorated with gold patterns and lots of gold jewellery. Tilak (red paste) is used to make the Bindi mark on her forehead (see page 52), and her hands and feet are decorated with elaborate Mendhi patterns made of henna (see page 52).

At the start of the wedding ceremony, the bride and groom sit facing one another under a colourful canopy called a Mandap. At first they may be hidden from each other's sight by a sheet held between them, but they are attached by a circular cord placed over their heads. The cord remains in place throughout the ceremony.

The family trees of the couple are read out, and prayers and mantras are chanted. The right hands of the bride and groom are sometimes tied together, and water that has been blessed is poured over them.

At some point in the ceremony, a sacred fire is lit. The couple perform Havan (see page 46), making offerings of ghee (clarified butter) and grains (symbolic of fertility) to the fire. Then the couple, walking side by side, take seven steps around the fire. This symbolises their journey together through life. The steps stand for: food, strength, wealth, good fortune, children, happiness throughout the seasons and friendship.

The wedding ceremony ends with a feast traditionally provided by the bride's parents.

DEATH

Beliefs

Hindus believe in reincarnation, sometimes called the transmigration of souls. They believe that when a person dies, the soul is reborn in a new body and has another earthly existence. The quality of one's state of rebirth depends upon the quality of one's moral behaviour in the previous life (see page 34). The soul has to go through many rebirths before Moksha (ultimate liberation–see page 35) can be achieved.

Customs

The belief in reincarnation emphasises that it is Atman (the soul) that is important, rather than the body. After death, the body is not needed any more and so it is cremated. The dead person's relatives stay at home throughout the period when the ceremonies associated with death are performed. During this time, they are not supposed to meet people or to have any contact with outsiders.

In India, the dead body is washed and wrapped in a cloth. The cremation takes place within a day of death, if possible. Traditionally, six male relatives carry the body in procession to the funeral pyre, a pile of wood, including sweet-smelling sandalwood. The eldest male relative of the deceased (usually the eldest son) lights the funeral pyre and ghee (clarified butter) is thrown on to the flames. Prayers and readings from the Bhagavad Gita are recited while the body burns.

Three days after the cremation, the ashes are collected and scattered onto a river. If possible, they will be scattered on to the waters of the River Ganges (this is often done at Varanasi–see page 31). In the West, where Hindu cremations are carried out in crematoria, the ashes of the deceased are often sent to India to be scattered on to the Ganges.

Eleven or thirteen days after cremation, Kriya takes place. The family make an offering of Pindas (*rice balls*) to the person who has just died. After this they can go outside, meet people and carry on with their normal lives.

PLACES OF WORSHIP

Below: *A typical Hindu temple plan.*

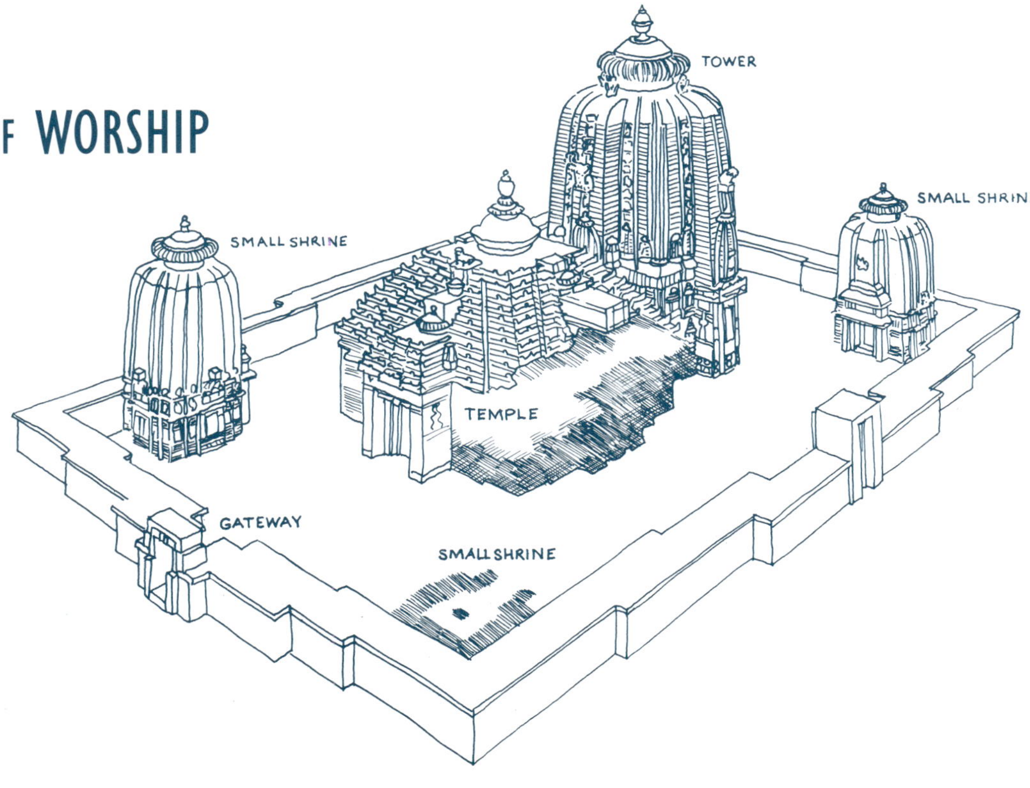

THE MANDIR

A Mandir is a Hindu temple. Most Mandirs in Britain are not purpose built, but like those in India they all have a worship hall containing statues and pictures of deities. The statues of the deities are washed, dressed and garlanded, and often they will be housed in shrines that are small versions of traditional Indian temples. The shrines may have offerings of food, flowers, money or fruit placed in front of them, and they are usually festooned with multicoloured tinsel and strings of small electric lights.

The Mandir can be visited at any time, but there are set times for communal worship (in Britain this usually takes place on weekday evenings and at weekends). Shoes are removed before entering the worship hall, and a bell is rung before worship. This alerts the deity to the worshipper's presence.

There are no seats in the worship hall. Men and women usually sit separately on the floor at either side of the hall. For communal worship, a square fire-altar is placed in front of the main shrine at the front of the hall. There is music, hand-clapping, chanting and singing.

Attached to every Mandir is a priest, supported by the local community, who officiates at congregational worship.

Above: *Praying to Shiva.*
Below: *Arti lamps .*

CONGREGATIONAL PUJA

There are three main elements in congregational Puja (*worship*): Havan, Arti and Bhajans.

Havan

Puja begins with Havan (offering of fire). Havan is also known as Agnihotra after Agni, the Vedic god of fire. The priest lights the fire and pours on ghee (clarified butter) while chanting passages from the scriptures. He then takes some water into his left hand, dips a finger of his right hand into it and touches his ears, nose, eyes, mouth, arms, body and legs. The other worshippers do the same, and prayers are offered to all the main gods.

Arti

During Arti a special lamp with five wicks is lit. The lamp is waved in front of the images of the deities and then, in order to receive their blessing, each person holds her/his hands over the flames and passes them over their own forehead and hair.

The five wicks of the Arti lamp are a reminder of the five elements of the universe, which are symbolised by different aspects of the Arti ceremony. Fire is represented by the lamp; earth is represented by incense and flowers; air is represented by the waving of a fan; water is contained in a conch shell, the blowing of which symbolises the fifth element, ether.

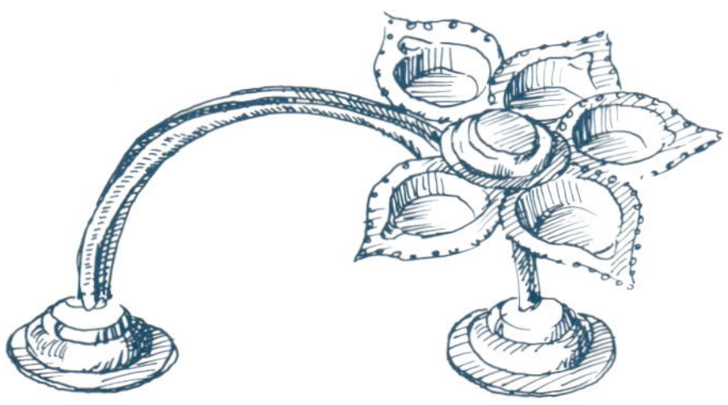

Before the end of Arti, a mixture of dried fruits, nuts and sugar crystals is distributed. This is Prashad, special food that has first been offered to the deities. Visitors to the Mandir are likely to be offered Prashad.

Bhajans

Bhajans (devotional hymns or songs) are sung and chanted whenever Hindus worship. They are accompanied by hand-clapping and the playing of percussion instruments. Often the fervour and enthusiasm generated will cause people to start dancing, which Hindus consider to be an entirely appropriate form of worship.

CENTRES OF PILGRIMAGE

Yatra (*pilgrimage*) is an important religious activity for Hindus. India is full of holy places and centres of pilgrimage. An old Hindu text lists the places that are the most conducive to worship. The list includes river banks, caves, mountain tops, confluences of rivers, sacred forests, solitary groves, valleys, islands, the sea shore, and lonely places free from animals.

The most famous pilgrimage centre is the city of Varanasi (formerly known as Banaras), which is situated on the banks of the River Ganges. Varanasi is sacred to the god Shiva, and Hindus come here to worship at the many temples and shrines and to bathe in the river. At the end of their lives many Hindus come to Varanasi to die and to have their ashes scattered on the holy waters.

Above: *Map showing some places of pilgrimage in India.*

The largest regular gathering of human beings at any one place in the world takes place every twelve years for Kumbha Mela, the greatest of all India's pilgrimage-festivals. Kumbh Mela takes place at the confluence of the River Ganges and the River Yamuna at Allahabad. Up to 15 million people bathe in the sacred waters during the five days of the festival.

RITUAL OBJECTS AND ARTEFACTS

IMAGES OF DEITIES

Brahma

Brahma is the Absolute creator of the universe, from which everything comes and to which everything returns. He has four faces, of which only three are visible. These represent the four Vedas (ancient scriptures) and enable him to look in every direction at once. His four arms represent the points of the compass, and in his four hands he carries a variety of objects. These include a water jug (a reminder of his function as the creator, since water is the source of all life); a spoon (representing the offerings made in worship); a sceptre; a bow; a book (the Vedas); a lotus; and prayer beads (representing time). He either rides a goose (symbol of wisdom), or stands or sits in the 'full lotus' posture on a large lotus.

Saraswati

Saraswati is the consort of Brahma. She is the goddess of learning and the arts. She is described as beautiful, with a milky white face and dressed in white. She has four arms representing mind, intellect, conscience and ego. With two of her hands she plays the vina (a stringed musical instrument resembling a sitar), and in the others she holds prayer beads and a book (the Vedas). Like Brahma, she either stands or sits on a lotus or rides a white goose. She may also be shown with a swan or a peacock.

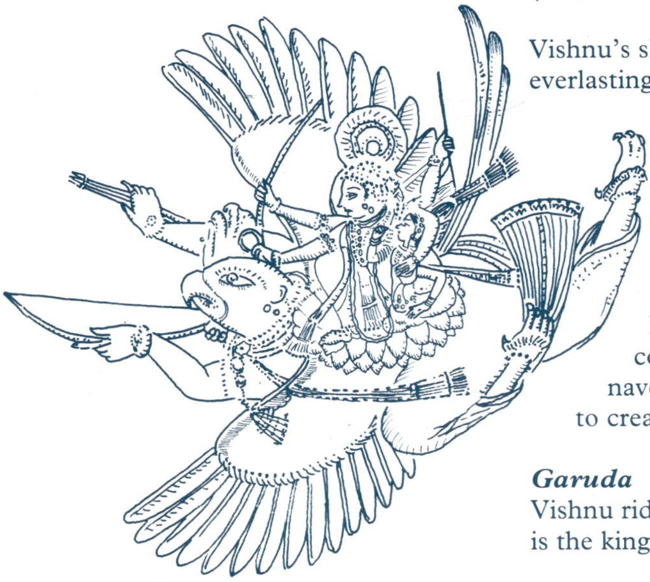

Vishnu
Vishnu preserves and sustains the universe and all forms of life within it. He also protects the world from evil, sometimes coming down to the earth in human form in order to do this. His two most celebrated Avatars (incarnations) are those of Rama and Krishna.

Vishnu's skin is blue because, like the sky, he is everywhere and he is everlasting. He has a distinctive mark upon his forehead, which is also worn by Vaishnavites (devotees of Vishnu). In his four hands he holds a lotus, a conch shell, a club and a chakra (a wheel representing the solar disc, the cycle of life and death, and a weapon).

Vishnu is often depicted sitting or lying in the coils of Ananta or Shesha, the thousand-headed serpent. As Vishnu Naryana he sleeps soundly in the serpent's coils on the infinite cosmic ocean. His consort Lakshmi sits at his feet, and from his navel a lotus blooms. In the lotus flower sits Brahma, who is about to create the world and the first human beings.

Garuda
Vishnu rides Garuda, a creature that is half man and half bird. Garuda is the king of the birds, and occasionally he is depicted as a bird.

Lakshmi
Lakshmi is the consort of Vishnu. She is the goddess of wealth, prosperity and happiness. When shown with Vishnu, she only has two arms. When shown alone, she has four. In two of her hands she holds lotus flowers. With her other hands she bestows gifts, including gold coins. Lakshmi stands or sits on a lotus, and sometimes has elephants on either side of her.

Above: *Vishnu and Lakshmi riding on Garuda, Bundi School 18th century.*

Rama
Rama is the seventh Avatar (incarnation) of Vishnu, and his story is told in the Ramayana (see page 38). Like Vishnu, he has blue skin and wears the mark of Vishnu on his forehead. He carries a bow and has a quiver full of arrows on his back. He is often shown with Sita, his wife (herself an avatar of Lakshmi) and Lakshmana, his brother, on either side, and with Hanuman, the monkey god, kneeling at his feet.

Hanuman
Hanuman, the monkey god, is the faithful friend and helper of Rama. He is revered for his devotion, loyalty and strength. He has the head of a monkey and a muscular human body. In one hand he carries a club, and in the other a mountain. The reason for this is that during the battle between the forces of Rama and those of Ravana, Lakshmana, Rama's brother, was seriously injured. Hanuman was sent to collect healing herbs from a mountainside, but when he got there he was unsure about which herbs to pick. To solve the problem, he simply picked up the entire mountain and carried it back to Lakshmana, thus saving his life.

Above: *Hanuman carrying Rama and Sita.*

Krishna
Krishna is the eighth Avatar (incarnation) of Vishnu. Krishna literally means black or blue-black (the colour of his skin). He carries a flute, bears the mark of Vishnu on his forehead and wears a peacock feather in his hair. He is often shown with a white cow, recalling his flirtatious exploits with the gopis (cowgirls).

Radha
Krishna is accompanied by Radha, his consort (herself an Avatar of Lakshmi). When Radha and Krishna are shown together, the image embodies the two aspects of the Divine (male and female), which together form the One.

The reciprocal love and devotion that exists between Krishna and Radha reflects that which exists between Krishna and his followers. The best-known group of devotees of Krishna belong to ISKCON – the International Society for Krishna Consciousness (sometimes inappropriately referred to as 'Hare Krishnas').

Shiva Dakshina-Murti / Shiva Mahayogi
Shiva is the god whose destructive Shakti (energy) paves the way for renewal. He is usually shown as Shiva Dakshina-Murti or Mahyogi, an ascetic sitting on top of the Himalayas deep in meditation. He sits in the 'full lotus' posture on a tiger skin or a lotus, wearing a simple loincloth or an antelope skin around his waist.

In Shiva's hair there is a crescent moon. At the top of his head there is either a fountain of water, representing the source of the River Ganges, or the face of Ganga, the river goddess. Snakes twist through his hair and entwine his neck.

Shiva has three eyes, to perceive the past, present and future, and he looks southwards, the direction that brings good luck. In his four hands he holds a trident (representing the Trimurti: Brahma, Vishnu and Shiva); a hand-drum (symbolising the original sound of creation); and a water jug (symbolising renewal).

The story behind the image of Shiva

A Rishi is a person who is spiritually wise. One would normally expect a Rishi to act with self-restraint, but on a particular occasion, 10,000 Rishis became so angry that they acted with great foolishness. The reason for their anger was that all of their wives had fallen in love with the handsome god Shiva.

In their jealous rage, the Rishis sent a wild tiger and then an antelope to attack Shiva, but he killed and skinned them with his bare hands. Shiva tamed the poisonous snakes which the Rishis sent, and wore them in his hair and around his neck. He caught the red hot iron and the crescent-shaped sickle that the Rishis hurled, making a weapon from the iron and using the moon sickle as an ornament in his hair. Finally, the Rishis sent an evil black dwarf to kill Shiva, but the god knocked the dwarf over and danced on his belly. Acknowledging Shiva's true greatness, the Rishis bowed down before him and worshipped him.

Shiva Nataraja
Shiva is often depicted as Shiva Nataraja (*the Lord of the Dance*). The universe and all that it contains are perceived to be participating in a great cosmic dance. The universe was set in motion by the regular rhythm of the dance, and the dance of the universe is the dance of Shiva.

Shiva dances in a circle of flames. The circle represents time, with no beginning or end. The flames symbolise Shakti (energy) in its purest form, and also serve as a reminder of the fires of cremation.

In one of Shiva's four hands he holds a small drum. The sound of the drum is the sound of creation. Sometimes Shiva stops playing the drum in order to find a new and better rhythm. At that moment the universe ends, to be recreated when the music restarts.

The palm of another hand holds fire, revealing Shiva's ability to destroy the universe. One hand flops down from an arm stretched across his body. This arm represents the trunk of an elephant, and the gesture symbolises strength.

Shiva's raised left foot represents Moksha (ultimate liberation), and his right foot treads on the dwarf of ignorance.

The Shiva Linga and Nandi

Paradoxically, Shiva is associated on the one hand with destruction and death, and on the other with fertility and procreation. The Shiva Linga and statues of bulls are characteristic features of shrines dedicated to Shiva. The Shiva Linga is a stylised representation of sexual congress, and the bull is a symbol of fertility. Shiva is often shown riding, or accompanied by, a white bull called Nandi.

Parvati

Shiva's consort is Parvati. She also appears as Durga and Kali, and in her is manifested Shakti (energy or power associated with Shiva). Shiva and Parvati are often shown together. Sometimes Parvati sits on Shiva's knee while he embraces her, sometimes they stand side by side, and sometimes they are depicted as lovers. As with Radha and Krishna, images of Parvati and Shiva together symbolise the union of the female and male aspects of the One Absolute.

Durga

Shakti (energy or power associated with Shiva) is manifested in the ferocious form of Durga (*the One who is Difficult to Approach*). Durga has eight arms and carries many weapons with which to combat evil demons, such as Mahishasura, the buffalo demon (see page 43). The objects in her eight hands include a trident, sword, snake, bell, drum, shield, skull bowl, bow and arrow, wheel, club, water jug and conch shell. Durga rides a lion or a tiger.

Kali

Shakti (energy or power associated with Shiva) is manifested in the terrifying form of Kali (*the Black One*). Kali is the embodiment of the force that brings time to an end. She symbolises the destruction of the world in order that it can be recreated. Kali devours everything in her path. Her tongue hangs out, dripping with the blood of her victims. She wears a necklace of skulls and severed arms hang from her waist. She holds a severed head in one of her four hands, and in another she wields a sickle. As Shiva's consort, she subjugates him completely and is often shown dancing on his body.

Ganesha

Ganesha, the elephant-headed god, is the popular son of Shiva and Parvati (see story on page 42). He is the god of good fortune and the remover of obstacles. Ganesha's large tummy symbolises the universe and acts as a reminder that earthly delights do not have to be an obstacle to profound spiritual insights. A snake is tied around his waist. In his four hands he holds a variety of objects including a noose (for catching elephants), a goad (for guiding elephants), one of his own tusks, and a dish of sweets which he sniffs with his trunk!

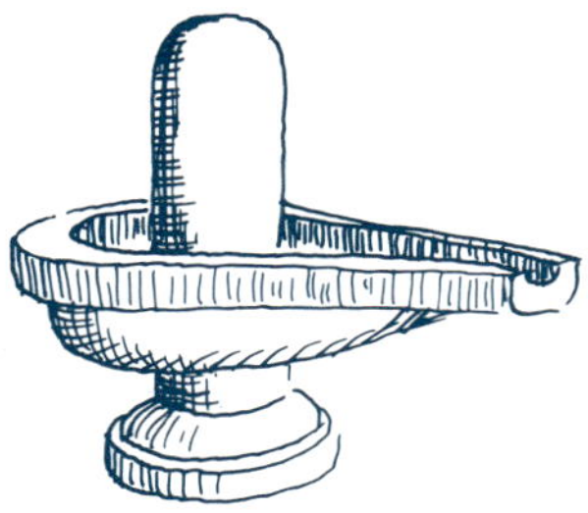

From the top: *Shiva Linga; Nandi; Shiva and Parvati; Kali.*

Ganesha sometimes dances a powerful cosmic dance, reminiscent of that of his father Shiva. He sits on a lotus throne with a rat at his feet. Sometimes the rat takes him for rides (see story below).

The story behind the image of Ganesha

One night, after eating far too many sweets, Ganesha went riding through the forest on the back of his companion, the rat. Suddenly, a snake slid out from the undergrowth and raised its head in front of the rat. The startled rat reared up and Ganesha fell from its back. Ganesha hit the ground with such force that his huge belly split wide open, and all the sweets that were inside tumbled out. Ganesha scooped all the sweets back into his tummy, grabbed the snake and tied it around his waist, using it to close the split in his stomach.

Now the sound of mocking laughter filled the night air. Looking up, Ganesha saw the full moon laughing at his misfortune. He was so angry that he tore off one of his own tusks and hurled it at the moon. The moon ducked down below the horizon, waited a few hours and then rose again into the sky. After a few more hours, the moon began to feel nervous and ducked back down under the horizon, only to emerge a few hours later.

PUJA TRAY

The Puja tray holds the offerings and objects used in Puja (*worship*) in the home (see page 36):

- A bell, which is rung at the start of Puja to alert the deities to the presence of the worshippers.
- A dish containing Tilak (sandalwood paste) used to mark the worshipper's forehead.
- Offerings of food such as rice, nuts, sweets and fruit, and flowers.
- A pot containing water used for cleansing and purification, and a spoon with which to pour the water.
- A Diva (lamp with one wick) or an Arti lamp (lamp with five wicks–see page 39), filled with ghee (clarified butter).
- An incense or joss stick holder.

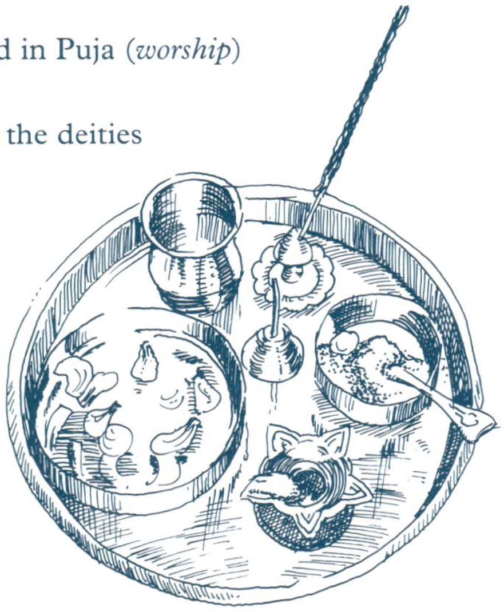

DIVAS

Divas are lamps. They are filled with ghee and have cotton wool wicks. The Divas used in Puja (*worship*–see pages 38 and 39) are made of metal and often have handles. The Divas used during the festival of Divali (see page 39) are made from small clay or earthenware bowls.

RAKHIS

Rakhis are decorated bracelets made of silk or cotton which sisters tie around their brothers' wrists during the festival of Raksha Bandhan (see page 41).

MALA BEADS

A Mala is a string of 108 prayer beads used while meditating on the names of the deities, especially those of Vishnu.

MENDHI PATTERNS

Mendhi patterns are elaborate henna patterns made on the hands and feet. Henna powder is mixed with warm water and lemon juice to make a paste (tubes of henna paste can also be bought). The paste is applied with a small stick, often through the holes of a plastic stencil, and when it is washed off an orange mark remains. The patterns are worn by Hindu, Sikh and Muslim women from the Indian sub-continent for important occasions such as their wedding day and for major festivals.

GARLANDS

Garlands may be brightly coloured and made of tinsel, or they may be made of sweet-smelling sandalwood shavings. They are used to decorate shrines and images of deities both at home and in the Mandir. They are worn at weddings (see page 44), and by the dead when they are cremated (see page 45).

BINDI

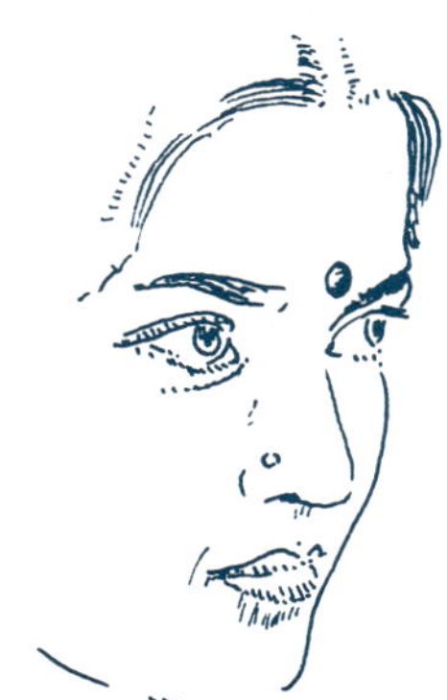

A Bindi is the mark placed on the foreheads of Hindu women. Traditionally, it is made from coloured powder and it has religious significance, being worn as a third eye to ward off evil, as a sign of dedication or as a sign that the wearer has been blessed. Today Bindis are often worn purely for personal decoration. They come in commercially produced 'stick on' form.

MANDALAS / YANTRAS

Mandalas or Yantras are circular geometric patterns used as a visual focus for meditation. The patterns serve to illustrate the essential unity and wholeness of all things.

SYMBOLS

AUM

Aum (sometimes spelt Om) is the most sacred of Hindu words. It is the sacred symbol and sound representing the ultimate. It is the sound that brings all of Creation into being, and it is chanted as a sacred Mantra during meditation.

A represents the creative power of Brahma.
U represents the sustaining power of Vishnu.
M represents the destructive power of Shiva.

SWASTIKA

The Swastika is an ancient symbol for good fortune. It often appears in connection with images of Hindu deities. The four arms of the Swastika signify three things:

The four directions (space).
The four Ashramas or stages in the life-cycle (time).
The four Vedas (knowledge).

(The Nazis adopted the Swastika as a symbol before World War II, which may cause some confusion.)

Islam

ALLAH IS MOST GREAT

I bear witness that there is no god but Allah

I bear witness that Muhammad is the messenger of Allah

Come to prayer

Come to success

Allah is most great

There is no god but Allah

From the Adhan (call to prayer)

Islam

BACKGROUND INFORMATION

MUHAMMAD

The prophet Muhammad was born in Makkah in 570 CE, shortly after the death of his father. His mother died when he was six and he went to live with his uncle, who was a trader. After travelling widely and broadening his experience, Muhammad himself became a trader. When he was 24 he began to work for a wealthy widow called Khadijah. A year later he married his employer.

Muhammad often left the city to seek peace in the desert. He liked to spend time alone in caves outside Makkah. In 610 CE, during one of these vigils, he received a revelation from the angel Jibril (*Gabriel*– see page 61). Jibril told Muhammad that Allah, the one true God (Allah means *the* God), had chosen him to be his messenger. Muhammad returned home to Khadijah, who convinced him that he had been chosen as a prophet.

Muhammad received further revelations from Jibril. The revelations were recorded by friends of Muhammad and eventually were collected together to form the Qur'an, the holy book of Islam. After the first revelation, for the remaining twenty or so years of his life, Muhammad preached about Allah, the One and Only God.

Muhammad gained a number of followers who joined him in the worship of Allah, but his message was not always well received. Makkah's wealth largely depended on the fact that it was a pilgrimage centre. Each year Arab tribes came to Makkah in order to worship at the Ka'bah, a cube-shaped building, filled with idols (the English word 'cube' comes from the Arabic 'Ka'bah'). When Muhammad criticised the people of Makkah for their religious practices, the merchants became incensed. Such criticism constituted a threat to their trade.

As opposition grew, the revelations that he received dwelt increasingly on the uniqueness of Allah. Muhammad was reminded of former prophets who had also encountered opposition, and of how Allah had saved them and brought downfall on their opponents. Among the stories revealed to Muhammad were those of Noah and the flood, Lot and the destruction of Sodom, and Moses and the Exodus.

Eventually the persecution suffered by Muhammad and his followers intensified to such an extent that their lives were in danger. In 622 CE they were forced to migrate from Makkah to Madinah. This event is known as Hijrah (*the departure, exit* or *emigration*), and Muslims date their calendar from this point in their history.

ORIGINS

Islam began in present-day Saudi Arabia in the 7th century CE. In Arabia at that time, there was widespread worship of various tribal gods and goddesses as well as a strong belief in one supreme God. In this mainly nomadic culture there was a mixture of beliefs: some tribes had absorbed Christian ideas, others followed Jewish traditions.

Muhammad (570-632 CE) established Islam in Arabia. Muslims never refer to him as the 'founder' of Islam because they consider Allah (*the God*) to be the true founder of their religion. Muhammad was the last in a line of prophets of Allah which included Adam, Nuh (*Noah*), Ibrahim (*Abraham*), Musa (*Moses*), Dawud (*David*), Sulayman (*Solomon*) and Isa (*Jesus*).

Muhammad succeeded in bringing religious and political unity to Arabia during his lifetime. After his death Islam spread east and west, and within 100 years an empire was created which remains largely intact today. From Morocco to Pakistan and beyond, there extends a chain of countries united by the religion, history, language and culture of Islam.

Above: *The Prophet Muhammad with the Archangel Jibril* (Gabriel) *meeting Musa* (Moses).
Left: *Muhammad as a religious and military leader facing enemy forces at Yathrib in 627 CE.*

A Hijrah Story

When Muhammad and his followers travelled from Makkah to Madinah, they were pursued by their enemies. A well-known story tells of how Muhammad and his friends hid in a cave. The people that were chasing them came right up to the entrance of the cave and peered inside. A dove was feeding her young just by the entrance, and across the mouth of the cave stretched an unbroken spider's web. Thinking that Muhammad and his followers could not possibly have entered the cave without disturbing the dove and breaking the spider's web, the people pursuing Muhammad left to look elsewhere.

Madinah was a fertile oasis whose people hoped that Muhammad would help them to heal the bitter rifts which existed within their community. They were prepared to accept Muhammad as a prophet, and he became both a religious and a political leader.

Conflict between the people of Madinah and those of Makkah was inevitable, and soon war broke out between the two communities. In 630 CE Muhammad returned with his followers to conquer Makkah without bloodshed. He destroyed all the idols that were housed in the Ka'bah and declared that from that moment the Ka'bah was to be used for the worship of Allah alone.

Muhammad died in 632 CE having established one of the world's great religions and having brought unity to the people of Arabia.

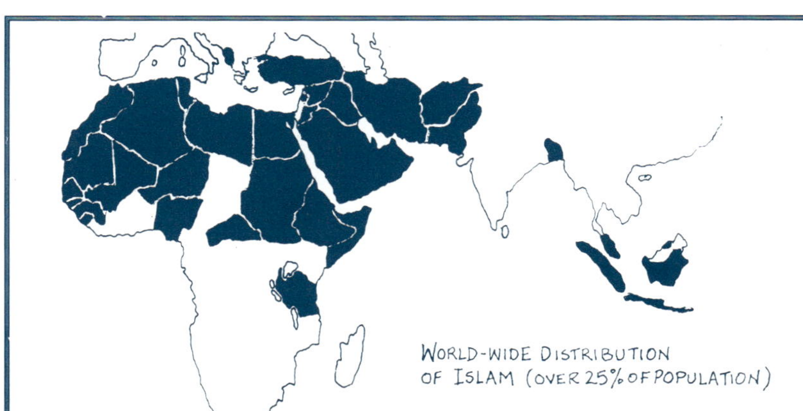

SUNNIS AND SHI'AHS

Over 80% of Muslims are Sunnis. They recognise the first four Caliphs (*Successors*) as true successors of Muhammad. The Shi'ahs, who are mainly concentrated in Iran and India, disregard the first three Caliphs as they were not related to Muhammad. They regard Muhammad's son-in-law Ali and his successors as divinely ordained Caliphs.

Above:
Abu Bakr (573-634 CE), acknowledged by Sunnis to be the first Caliph.

SUFIS

Sufism is a mystical offshoot of Islam. Sufis, who are proportionately very small in number, perform various spiritual practices including meditating and reciting the names of Allah. They often use both music and dance in their rituals. Members of the Turkish Mevlevi order (often incorrectly called Whirling Dervishes) perform the Sema, a swirling, spinning dance evoking the rotation of the planets around the sun.

MUSLIMS TODAY

With a global population approaching 1,300 million, Islam is second only to Christianity in terms of numbers of adherents. There are approximately 1,500,000 Muslims in Britain. Around two-thirds of British Muslims have family origins in the Indo-Pakistan sub-continent, coming to Britain either directly or via East Africa or the Caribbean.

Muhammad's night journey

The well-known story of al-Isra (Muhammad's night journey to Jerusalem) and al-Miraj (his subsequent ascension into heaven) is very significant for Muslims.

One night as Muhammad slept, the angel Jibril (*Gabriel*) appeared and spoke: '*Arise Muhammad and come*'.

Muhammad followed Jibril outside, where a winged animal similar to a horse but with a human face was waiting. This was the magical and mysterious creature called Buraq.

No sooner had Muhammad mounted Buraq than he found himself transported in an instant from Makkah to Jerusalem. In the Aqsa mosque were assembled all the prophets who had gone before, and Muhammad led them in prayer. He then visited the sacred rock upon which Ibrahim had nearly sacrificed Isma'il his son (see page 64).

From the rock, Muhammad ascended with Jibril and other angels into the seven heavens, where he met various prophets including Musa (*Moses*), Isa (*Jesus*), Ibrahim (*Abraham*) and Adam. Muhammad then journeyed beyond the seventh heaven, into a realm where he was able to see and comprehend things that were normally beyond human sight and understanding. Here, in the presence of Allah, time stood still and space had no meaning.

And then Muhammad found himself back in Makkah, where he sat until dawn, quietly reflecting on all that he had experienced that night.

Right: *The ascent of the Prophet. From a manuscript Khanseh, by Nizama, Shiraz, Iran. Note that unusually the face of Muhammad is shown.*

BELIEFS AND WAY OF LIFE

ALLAH

Muslims believe that Allah (*the God*) is One. Belief in the Oneness of Allah, the essence of Islam, is known as Tawhid.

The word Islam denotes a state of peace attained through willing obedience to Allah's divine guidance. A Muslim is one who submits himself or herself completely to Allah. Some Muslims repeat the following words many times during the day, whenever an important action is performed:

'Bismillah ir-Rahman ir-Rahim.'

(In the name of God, the Compassionate, the Merciful.)

According to the Qur'an, Allah has 99 known names, including the Compassionate, the Merciful, the First, the Last, the Almighty, the Creator, the Giver of Life, the Provider, the Guide, the Forgiver and the Judge.

AL-MU'MIN
The Guardian of Faith
(He who places faith in the heart of his servants, protects those whe seek refuge in Him, and gives tranquility).

Above: *One of the 'Ninety-nine names of Allah'.*

ANGELS

Belief in angels is a very important aspect of Islam. Whereas humans possess freewill and therefore have the capacity to disobey Allah, angels are always obedient to Allah and will not have to face judgement on the Last Day (see page 66). They carry out the will of Allah, which includes acting as Allah's messengers and bringing revelations to the prophets (see page 57).

SHARI'AH LAW

Muslim beliefs are put into practice through obedience to the Shari'ah (Islamic law). The Shari'ah covers all aspects of life, including religious rituals, family life, economics and the behaviour of rulers.

Allah has made certain things Haram (unlawful). Everything else is Halal (lawful). Meat is Halal if it is slaughtered according to Shari'ah laws. All seafood is Halal. Pork is Haram, as are alcoholic drinks.

Muslims are required to dress modestly. For men, this means covering at least from the knee to the navel; for women, it means covering the whole body except the face and the hands.

THE FIVE PILLARS

Islam requires its adherents to carry out certain duties which are expressions of basic beliefs. There are five particular requirements which support the Muslim way of life. These are known as 'The Five Pillars of Islam':

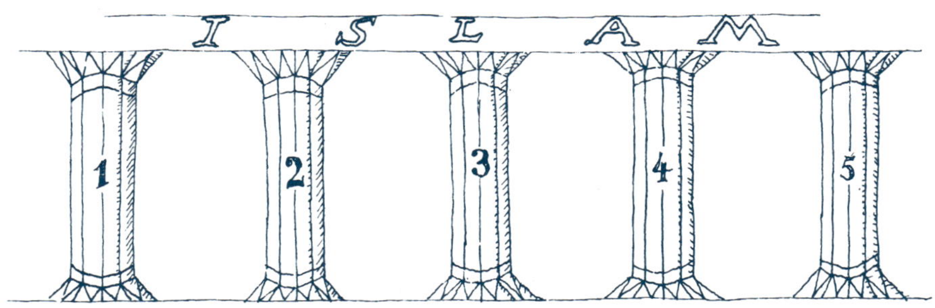

Shahadah declaration of faith	**Salah** prayer	**Zakah** giving	**Sawm** fasting	**Hajj** pilgrimage

Top: *Angel Jibril* (Gabriel) *from the pages of 'the Wonders of Creation of Qazvini', Iraq 14th century.*
Above: *The inscription on the vase reads:* 'There is no god except Allah, and Muhammad is the messenger of Allah'.
Below: *A Muezzin calls the faithful to prayer.*

The First Pillar – ***SHAHADAH*** *(declaration of faith):*
To be a Muslim one must believe the Shahadah: 'La ilaha illal Lahu Muhammadur rasulullah' ('*There is no god except Allah, and Muhammad is the messenger of Allah*').

The Second Pillar – ***SALAH*** *(communication with and worship of Allah):*
The aim of regular worship is to develop love for and devotion to Allah. There is a Muslim saying that prayer is like a refreshing stream into which one dips five times a day. Muslims have a duty to pray five times a day at set times and in set sequences.

In Muslim countries, the Mu'adhin or Muezzin (caller) calls the people to prayer from the top of a minaret, a slender tower attached to a Masjid (mosque).

The following words are taken from the Adhan (the call to prayer):

Allah is most great
I bear witness that there is no god but Allah
I bear witness that Muhammad is the messenger of Allah
Come to prayer
Come to success
Allah is most great
There is no god but Allah

Before prayer, shoes are removed and Wudu (ritual washing) is performed. Wudu is an elaborate ritual following a set sequence:

1 *Niyyah (intention)*
2 *Hands and wrists washed three times*
3 *Mouth washed three times*
4 *Nostrils washed out three times*
5 *Face washed three times*
6 *Arms up to elbows washed three times*
7 *Head, neck, and ears wiped once*
8 *Feet washed three times.*

Muslims always face the Ka'bah when they pray. A Qiblah compass may be used to establish the direction of Makkah (see page 68).

Prayers are said in Arabic in any clean place. A Musalla (prayer carpet) is often used to provide a clean surface on which to pray (see page 68).

Male muslims are expected to attend the Masjid (mosque) for Jumu'ah (Friday midday prayer).

During set prayers a particular sequence of movements, involving standing, bowing and prostrations, is followed. Each complete cycle of words and movements is called a Rak'ah. The sequence is as follows:

1 After Niyyah (statement of intent), Muslims stand with hands outstretched on either side of head and say: *'Allahu Akbar'* (*'Allah is most great'*). Saying 'Allahu Akbar' is called Takbir.
2 The right hand is placed over the left on the chest. Al-Fatihah (the opening Surah of the Qur'an, see page 61) and other passages of the Qur'an praising Allah are recited.
3 Muslims bow down, placing their hands upon their knees. They say three times: *'Glory be to my Great Lord, and praise be to him'.*
4 They stand and praise Allah.
5 They prostrate themselves fully, touching their foreheads on the ground. They say three times: *'Glory be to my Lord, the Most High. Allah is greater than all else'.*
6 They kneel with palms resting on knees. They may repeat three times: *'O my Master forgive me'.*
7 They prostrate themselves fully, touching their foreheads on the ground. They say three times: *'Glory be to my Lord, the Most High. Allah is greater than all else'.*
8 Muslims either repeat the Rak'ah, starting with **1** above, or they finish with a series of prayers. The last action is to turn the head to the right and left while kneeling and to speak the words: *'Peace be with you, and the mercy of Allah'.*

Above: *Muhammad washes his hands before prayer, a tradition which Muslims have followed to the present day.*
Below: *Muslim prayer positions.*

1 **2**

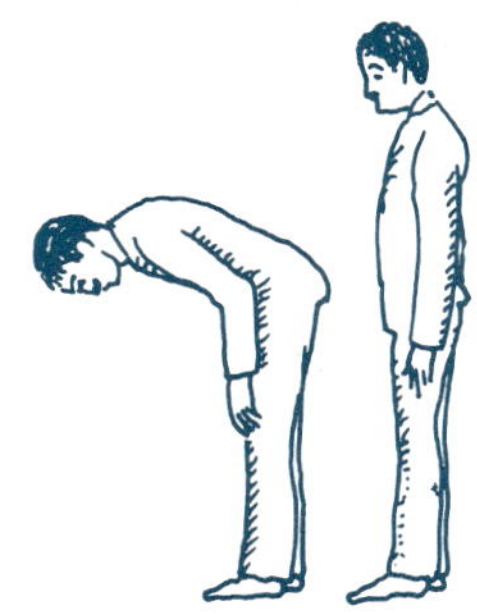

3 **4**

5 **6**

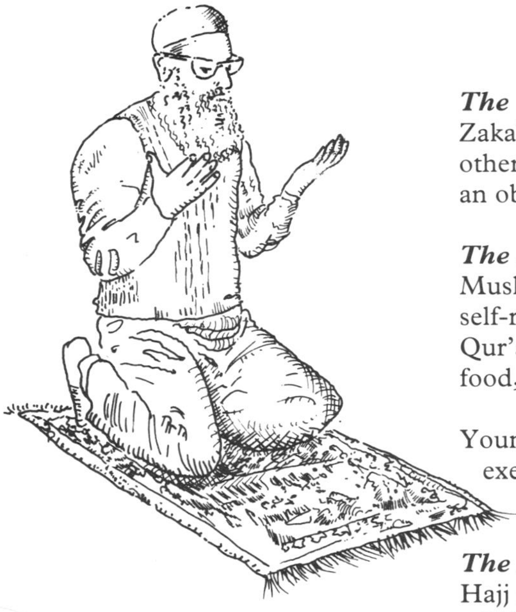

The Third Pillar*– *ZAKAH* *(annual welfare due)
Zakah is a proportion of one's wealth (2.5% of annual savings and other items) given to the needy, as defined in the Qur'an. It is both an obligation and an act of worship.

The Fourth Pillar*– *SAWM* *(fasting)
Muslims fast during the month of Ramadan as a means of learning self-restraint. It is a time when they remember the revelation of the Qur'an to Muhammad. From daybreak until sunset they abstain from food, drink, smoking and sexual relations.

Young children, pregnant women, people who are ill and travellers are exempt. Those who are sick or who are travelling can make up for lost days later on.

The Fifth Pillar*– *HAJJ* *(pilgrimage)
Hajj is the annual pilgrimage to the Ka'bah in Makkah during the month of Dhul Hijjah. Muslims who are healthy and can afford to do so have a duty to participate in the Hajj at least once during their lifetime. A man who completes the pilgrimage is called a Haji. A women who completes the pilgrimage is called a Hajiah. To show the complete equality of all Muslims, male pilgrims wear Ihram, two white unsewn sheets of cloth. Women wear normal Islamic dress.

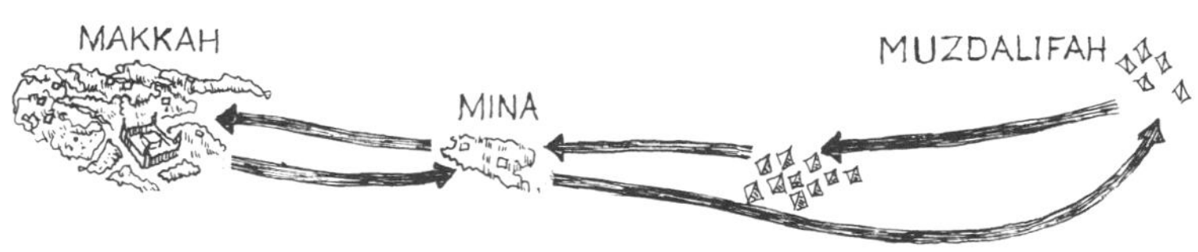

As soon as the pilgrims arrive in Makkah, whether during the day or at night, they make their way to the Ka'bah and walk seven times around it. As they pass one corner of the cube-shaped building, they try to touch the Black Stone, which is believed to have been given to Isma'il (*Ishmael*, Abraham's son) by the Angel Jibril (*Gabriel*).

A long covered walkway is incorporated into the mosque that has been built around the Ka'bah. This links two small hills, Safa and Marwah. Hajar, the wife of Ibrahim (*Abraham*), ran frantically between these two hills in a desperate search for water, only to discover that Isma'il, her son, had dug his toes into the sand as he lay dying, and had found water at the well of Zamzam. The pilgrims perform Sa'y, hurrying seven times along the walkway between Safa and Marwah, before visiting the Zamzam well.

Top: *Prayer on the Musalla (prayer carpet).*
Above: *During Ramadan, Muslims eat a light meal before dawn, then fast all day until sunset.*
Below: *The Ka'bah in Makkah.*

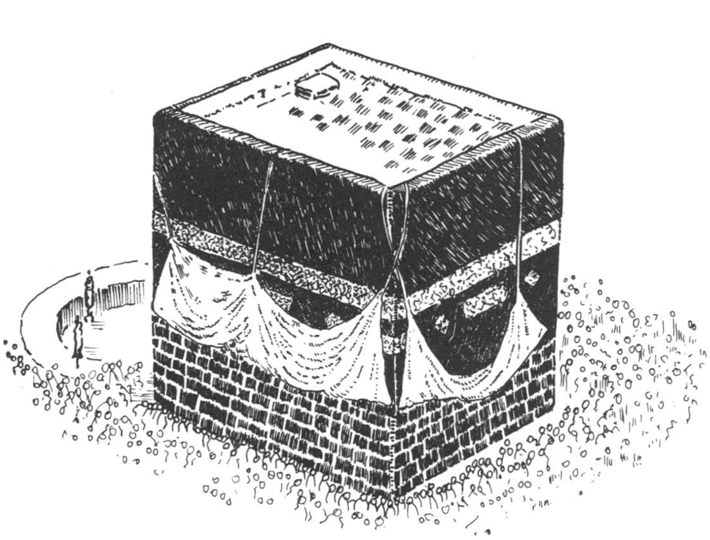

After camping at Mina, the pilgrims travel to the plain of Arafat and gather around the Mount of Mercy, where Muhammad delivered his last sermon. From noon until sunset, all the pilgrims (up to two million of them) stand in quiet meditation and prayer.

The pilgrims return to Mina after spending a night at Muzdalifah, where they each collect pebbles. At Mina, the pilgrims stone the Devil by hurling the pebbles at three Jamras (stone pillars).

The Hajj ends when the pilgrims return to Makkah to walk seven times more around the Ka'bah. Many of the pilgrims stay on to visit the Masjid (mosque) in Madinah which contains Muhammad's tomb.

VISUAL ART

Muslims consider that it is offensive to Allah to attempt to reproduce anything which Allah has created. Representational art has sometimes been used, for instance in the fine arts traditions of Persia and the Moghul empire, but depictions of Allah and Muhammad have never been permitted in Islam.

As a direct result of these restrictions, highly sophisticated forms of abstract art and design have been developed, characterised mainly by the use of patterns. The three main types of pattern are used in Islamic art are arabesque, geometric and calligraphy.

*Swirling flowery and leafy patterns, called **arabesque**, are used to convey something of the nature of paradise, which is understood to resemble a beautiful garden. The word 'paradise' comes from the Persian word 'pardis' which means garden.*
Ceramic tile, Topaki Palace, Turkey.

***Geometric** designs are used to convey the order, beauty and inter-relatedness of the natural world that Allah has created. The fact that these designs are endless indicates the infinite nature of Allah.*
Tile decoration in Bedi Palace, Marakesh, Morocco.

***Calligraphy** is used in a variety of imaginative ways to convey the beauty of the writings contained in the Qur'an.*
Frontispiece from 15th century manuscript, Mevlana Mosque, Turkey.

It is also offensive to Allah for anyone to attempt to make anything that is flawless: only Allah can create perfection and it is extremely arrogant for humans to attempt to do the same. Hence the idea that a Muslim artist or craftsperson will always make a deliberate mistake.

WRITINGS

THE QUR'AN

(see also page 68)

The Qur'an is believed to be the actual word of Allah, revealed to Muhammad by the angel Jibril (*Gabriel*). As such, the Qur'an is treated with great respect and looked to as the source of authority and inspiration.

The Qur'an was first revealed to Muhammad when he was alone meditating in the desert. One night in a cave on Mount Hira a mysterious figure appeared before him. He squeezed Muhammad in a tight embrace and commanded him to read. Muhammad explained that he could not. The figure pressed him a second and third time, until Muhammad asked what he should read. Then the figure spoke the words:

> *'Read, in the name of your Lord, who created,*
> *Created man from a clot of blood.*
> *Read, for your Lord is bountiful,*
> *Who taught by the pen,*
> *Taught man what he knew not.'* (From Surah 96 of the Qur'an)

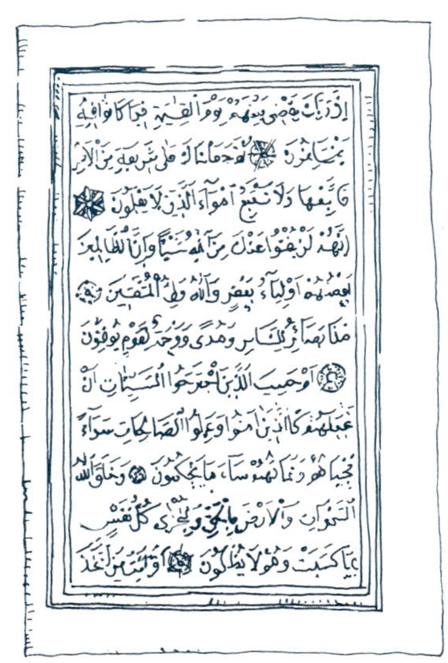

***Above:** A page from the Qur'an*

The figure spoke again saying: '*Muhammad you are the prophet of Allah and I am Jibril*'. Muhammad was terrified and returned immediately to Khadija, his wife, who reassured him. This first revelation took place on Laylat-ul-Qadr (*the Night of Power*), which occurs during Ramadan (see page 60).

Sometime later, the revelations continued and Muhammad's wife and friends began to write down the words that would eventually make up the Qur'an on anything that came to hand. After Muhammad's death, the final version of the Qur'an was copied 'from pieces of paper, stones, palm leaves, shoulder-blades, ribs, bits of leather and from the hearts of men'.

The Qur'an is divided into 114 Surahs (chapters). The Surahs do not appear in the order in which they were revealed to Muhammad. With the exception of the first Surah, Al-Fatihah (*the Opener*), the chapters are arranged with the longer ones first and the shorter ones at the end. Al-Fatihah, known as 'the Essence' of the Qur'an, is recited at least 17 times daily during Salah.

Above: *Angels are the messengers of Allah. The angel Jibril (*Gabriel*) told Muhammad that he was the prophet of Allah.*
Below: *Adam and Eve from a manuscript of Manafi al Hayawan, Iran, 1294-99.*
Bottom right: *A boy reads the Qur'an on a wooden stand.*

Many of the people and stories that appear in the Bible also appear (in different versions) in the Qur'an. Ibrahim (*Abraham*), Musa (*Moses*), Isa (*Jesus*), and Maryam (*Mary*, Jesus' mother) all feature prominently, along with other prophets common to Islam, Christianity and Judaism.

The Qur'an is written entirely in Arabic and, regardless of its religious significance, it is considered to be a great work of literature. Something of its beauty, poetry, majesty and power is inevitably lost in translation, and for Muslims a translation of the Qur'an can never be considered an authentic Qur'an, for Allah chose to reveal its contents in Arabic.

In Britain, most mosques organise classes at which children learn the Qur'an. They do this by reciting sections of the Qur'an out loud in Arabic until the words are memorised (the word Qur'an actually means 'that which is read or recited'). Learning to recite the whole of the Qur'an by heart is considered to be an act of great devotion. Many Muslim children do this and in recognition of their achievement they are given the title Hafiz.

Copies of the Qur'an are treated with great reverence. The book is wrapped in cloth and kept on a shelf above all other books. It is never touched with unwashed hands and it will usually be placed on a special wooden stand to be read.

THE HADITH AND THE SIRAH

The Hadith is the record of Muhammad's sayings, his actions, and the matters to which he consented. The Sirah is the biography of Muhammad's life. Together they provide an example of perfect behaviour for Muslims to follow in their daily lives, and are known as the Sunnah. The Sunnah together with the Qur'an form a complete source of guidance, and are the basis of Islamic law.

SUFI LITERATURE

The Islamic mystical movement known as Sufism is rich in poetry and story. Sufi teachers have always made use of parables and fables. 'The Conference of the Birds', by the 12th century Persian poet Attar, is a well-known allegory about the quest for the truth within. The blend of humour and insight which characterises Sufi stories about Mulla Nasrudin, the 'wise fool' of Turkish folklore, gives them a universal appeal.

FESTIVALS

Muslims use a lunar calendar. In an Islamic year there are 12 lunar months, each one lasting from one new moon to the next (29 or 30 days). This means there are 354 or 355 days in an Islamic year. The fact that the Muslim year is 10 or 11 days shorter than the Western, solar year means that from a Western perspective, each Muslim festival takes place 10 or 11 days earlier than it did the previous year. It also means that Muslim festivals are not associated with particular seasons. In a sense, they move 'backwards' through the seasons. The traditional festival greeting is 'Id Mubarak!' ('Id Greetings!').

Muharran, Safar, Rabi I, Rabi II, Jumad I, Jumad II, Rajab, Shaban, Ramadan, Shawwal, Dhu al Qa'dah, Dhul Hijja

Muharran: *New year* Day of Hijrah. The Islamic year starts on the day of Muhammad's departure from Makkah to Medinah in 622AD

Rabi I: *The birth of the Prophet in 570CE*

Shaban: *Laila al-Bar'h* The Night of Forgiveness in preparation for Ramadan

Ramadan: *Ramadan* A month of fasting in day-light hours

Lailat al-Qadr The Night of Power

Shawwal: *Id ul-Fitr* A joyful festival marking the end of Ramadan

Dhul Hijja: *Dhul Hijja* The month of pilgrimage to Makkah

Id ul-Adha The festival of sacrifice of meat for the poor, marking the end of Hajj

Above: *Detail from 'The Conference of the Birds', Iran 17th century.*
Below: *Muslims celebrating Id-ul Fitr, embracing each other at the festival.*

ID-UL-FITR

Id-ul-Fitr marks the end of Ramadan (the month of fasting). When the new moon is sighted, the month of fasting comes to an end and everyone celebrates. Id cards are given, presents such as boxes of sweets are exchanged, and new or best clothes are worn.

There is a special service in the morning in large Masjids (*mosques*) or wide open spaces. The whole family usually attends. At the Masjid, there is food and an opportunity to give generously to charity. There are big meals for families, neighbours and friends, and visits to the cemetery to remember the deceased. Throughout the day there is an emphasis on community, togetherness and sharing.

ID-UL-ADHA

Id-ul-Adha is a major four-day festival celebrating the end of the Hajj (the annual pilgrimage to Makkah–see page 60), and commemorating Ibrahim's willingness to sacrifice his son Isma'il for Allah (see the story below). Lambs or sheep are sacrificed with their heads held towards Makkah. A third of the meat is given to the poor, the rest is shared between family and friends. New or best clothes are worn for the festival, and Id cards and presents are given.

As at Id-ul-Fitr, there is a special service in the morning in large Masjids (mosques) or wide open spaces. The whole family usually attends.

The story behind Id-ul-Adha

The prophet Ibrahim (*Abraham*) once dreamt that he was ordered by Allah to sacrifice the thing that was most precious to him. There was nothing more precious to Ibrahim than Isma'il (*Ishmael*), his young son. When he told the boy of his dream, Isma'il calmly told his father that he must comply with Allah's command. Ibrahim told his son to bring a cord and a knife and together they climbed Mount Tabir.

At the top of the hill Isma'il spoke these words to his father: 'Tie my hands and feet and lie me face down on this rock. If you were to look at my face, your love for me might stop you from doing what you must do'. The rock on which Isma'il lay forms part of the Temple Mount in Jerusalem. A beautiful Islamic building with a golden dome has been built around it. This building is called the Dome of the Rock and it is the third holiest shrine in Islam, after the Ka'bah and the Prophet's Mosque in Madinah. Ibrahim was just about to perform the sacrifice when Allah spoke to him, telling him that he had been given something else to sacrifice instead of his son. Ibrahim opened his eyes and saw a big ram. He and Isma'il caught the ram and sacrificed it to Allah.

Left: *The Dome of the Rock is sacred to Muslims for three reasons: in memory of Abraham, who went to Mount Tabir to sacrifice his son; because of Solomon's Temple, whose Holy of Holies stood upon this spot; and because the prophet Muhammad had been carried from there on his 'night journey' (see page 57).*

RITES OF PASSAGE

BIRTH

Birth and Aqiqa

As soon as a new-born baby has been washed, the father or the Imam (prayer *leader*) whispers the Adhan (the call to prayer–see page 59) into the child's right ear and the Iqamah, containing almost the same words as the Adhan, into the child's left ear.

When the baby comes home, a small piece of sugar, a date or honey is placed in the child's mouth and a prayer is said. This ceremony is called Tahneek.

Seven days after birth, Aqiqa takes place. The baby's head is shaved and the hair is weighed. Gold or silver of an equal weight to the hair is given to the poor. If the baby is a boy, two goats or sheep are then sacrificed. If the baby is a girl, just one goat or sheep is sacrificed. The meat is cooked and eaten; one third is given to the relatives and two thirds to the poor.

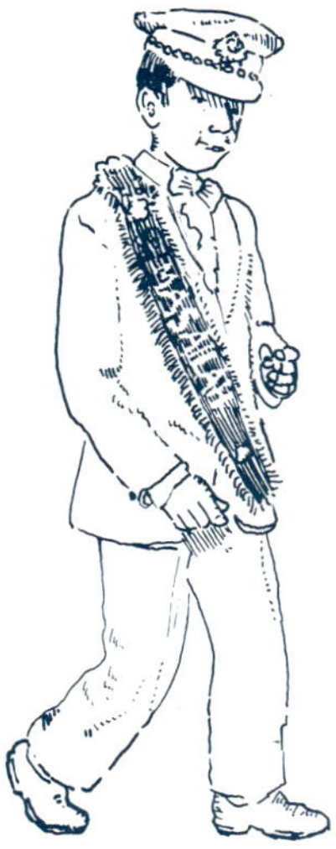

Above: *A Turkish boy before Khitan*

COMING OF AGE

Khitan and coming of age

Khitan (circumcision) is not required by the Qur'an, but all male Muslims have their foreskins removed in accordance with the practice of the prophets. Khitan is often performed at the time of Aqiqa, but it can take place at any time before the age of 10 is reached. In Turkey, boys are circumcised when they are eight or nine years old. Family parties are held, and boys who are about to be circumcised are dressed in white uniforms with red sashes.

There is no initiation ceremony in Islam. To be a Muslim is to believe the words of the Shahadah (the Muslim declaration of faith–see page 58) and to live one's life in total obedience to Allah. Children learn the customs and teachings of Islam in the home and at the Masjid (mosque). By the age of 12 or 13 they should be able to carry out their religious duties as adults.

MARRIAGE

Muslims are usually expected to marry within the religion and in most cases marriages are arranged between the families involved. The bride and groom have the right to refuse the person chosen for them and the wedding will not take place if the two partners do not agree to it. When the engagement is formally announced, the families of the couple exchange gifts and the groom presents Mahr (a dowry) to his bride.

In Muslim countries, weddings generally take place in the bride's family home. If the bride is from Pakistan or Bangladesh, she will probably wear red shalwar (trousers) and kameez (tunic) and plenty of gold jewellery. Her hands and feet will be decorated with patterns made from Mendhi (henna). When the groom arrives, he is welcomed by the bride's family and given garlands of flowers to wear. The bride and groom, with their respective parties, remain in separate rooms throughout the wedding ceremony.

In Britain, Muslim weddings usually take place at the Masjid (*mosque*). The Imam (prayer *leader*) does not have to be present. There is no set

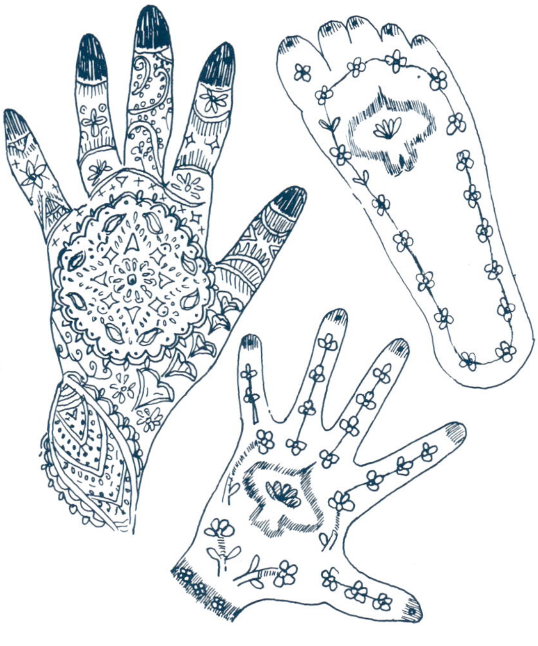

Above: *Examples of Mendhi patterns.*

order of service, but typically there are readings from the Qur'an and vows are said in front of witnesses. The couple always sign three copies of the Aqd Nikah (marriage contract): one for the bride, one for the groom and one to be kept by officials. The ceremony is followed by a wedding feast.

Under Islamic law, Muslim men are permitted to marry up to four wives provided they are treated equally well. Today, men often promise not to marry a second wife when they first marry.

Divorce is permitted in Islam, but only as the last resort. The divorce procedure follows a set pattern, allowing time for reconciliation.

DEATH

Beliefs

Belief in Akhirah (everlasting life after death) is of fundamental importance to Muslims. The Qur'an relates how, on the Last Day, the earth will be destroyed and the dead will come back to life to be judged by Allah. The good will reside joyfully in Paradise, living eternally in the presence of Allah. The damned will live forever in a place of everlasting fire and torment.

Customs

Dying Muslims are surrounded by family and friends, who read out passages from the Qur'an concerned with the afterlife. If possible, the last words that a Muslim speaks will be those of the Shahadah (the declaration of faith–see page 58). After death, the body is treated with great respect. It is washed three times, starting with the parts of the body washed before prayer during Wudu (see page 59). It is then perfumed and wrapped in three pieces of white cotton (or in Ihram if the dead person is a Haji–see page 60).

Top: *A Muslim wedding, Pakistan.*
Above: *Death of Muhammad.*
Below: *A Muslim funeral.*

The Qur'an teaches that on the Last Day the bodies of the dead will be restored, and for this reason Muslims are not permitted to be cremated. Funerals take place soon after death. At the burial, prayers are said, during which those present remain standing, and al-Fatihah (the first Surah of the Qur'an) is recited. The body is placed in the grave in such a way that the dead person's face is turned to the right, facing Makkah. The grave is raised a little above the ground. A simple headstone bears the name of the person who lies there, but elaborate monuments are forbidden. After burial, it is believed that angels visit the grave to question the deceased about their fitness for the next life.

Women rarely attend burials, but will visit the graves of family and friends for years afterwards. There is a period of mourning, but Muslims try not to be excessive in showing their grief.

PLACES OF WORSHIP

THE MASJID

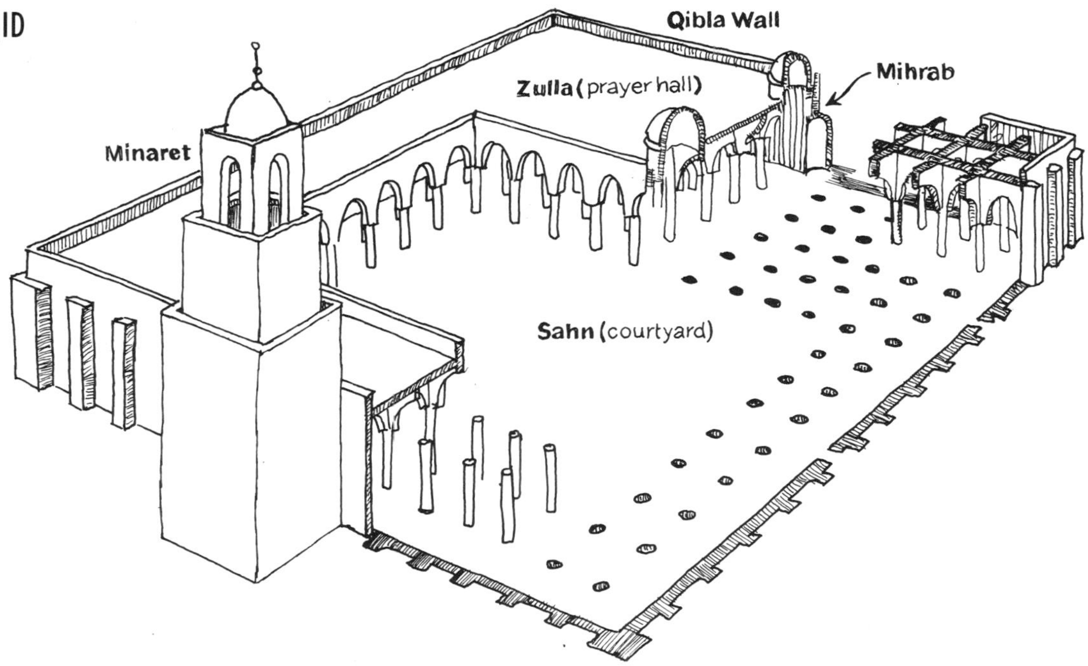

Masjid (*Place of Prostration*) is the correct Arabic term for a mosque. Most Masjids have three obvious features; at least one minaret, a washing area and a prayer hall. There may also be other rooms or areas set aside for a variety of purposes. These may include a classroom, a library, a meeting-room, a kitchen and a mortuary.

The minaret is the tower from which the Adhan (the call to prayer) is given (see page 59). The washing area is used for Wudu (see page 59). The prayer hall is a large carpeted area containing no seats and little furniture. It is often surmounted by a dome that enhances the sense of spaciousness. There are no pictures or statues, but the walls, the ceilings and the interior of the dome are often beautifully decorated with calligraphy, geometric designs and arabesque (see page 61).

The Qiblah is the direction of the Ka'bah in Makkah. The wall that the congregation faces inside the prayer hall is called the Qiblah wall, because to face it is to look towards Makkah. In the centre of the Qiblah wall is the Mihrab, an empty niche or alcove. To one side of the Mihrab is the Minbar, a dais from which the Imam (prayer *leader*) delivers the Khutbah (speech) on special occasions such as Jumu'ah (Friday midday prayer).

There is often a series of clock faces on one of the walls. These show the five times for daily prayer; the time for Jumu'ah and sometimes the times to begin and end fasting during Ramadan. Men generally pray at the front of the prayer hall and women pray either at the back or upstairs in a separate area. Many women pray at home, but men are expected to attend the Masjid, especially for Jumu'ah.

It is important to dress appropriately for a visit to a Masjid. Clothing should be clean. Males should wear long trousers, and although it is not obligatory, many also wear hats or Tigiyas (crocheted skullcaps– see page 68). Females should wear headscarves and long skirts or long trousers, and their arms should be covered. Shoes should be removed before entering the prayer hall.

Above left: *Minaret of the Great Mosque Kairouan, Tunisia, 9th century.*
Above right: *Ottoman minaret of the mosque of the Tekke of Mevlama Rumi in Konya, Turkey, 16th century.*

Above: Five clocks outside the Sama Masjid (mosque) in India show the times of daily prayer. The sixth clock is for Friday prayers, which are communal.

RITUAL OBJECTS AND ARTEFACTS

QUR'AN AND STAND

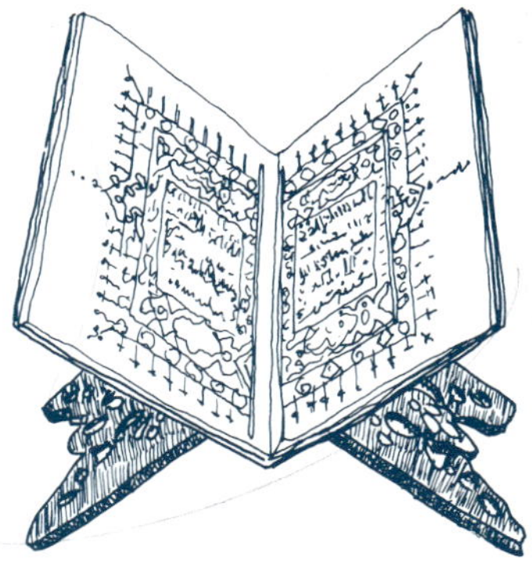

An authentic Qur'an will be written entirely in Arabic, without any translation. Arabic reads from right to left. The pages will be decorated with many beautiful and intricate patterns, but there will be no illustrations (see page 61).

In order not to cause offence, copies of the Qur'an should be treated respectfully and handled carefully. They should be wrapped in cloth and kept apart from other books in a secure place.

To keep the Qur'an off the floor when it is being read, it is placed on a special stand. The stand is made from a single piece of wood, often intricately carved.

PRAYER

Musalla

The Musalla (prayer carpet) is used outside the Masjid (mosque) to ensure that a clean surface is provided upon which to pray. Musallas are characterised by intricate patterns and beautiful colours, and they sometimes incorporate pictures of the Ka'bah and famous mosques into their design.

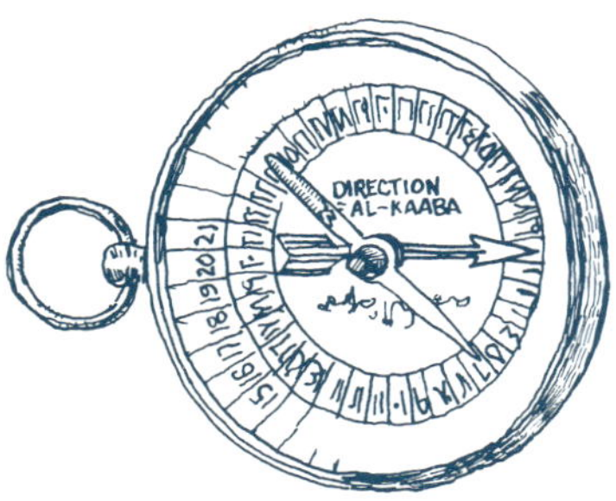

Qiblah Compass

Muslims must face Makkah during prayer, so if they are in an unfamiliar location, they use a special compass to establish the Qiblah (direction of Makkah). Qiblah compasses are sometimes fixed to Musallas (prayer carpets).

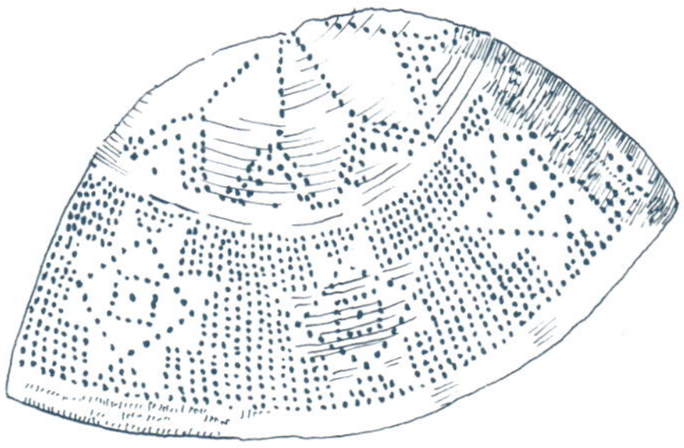

Tigiya

The Tigiya is a white crocheted skullcap. It is worn by many male Muslims when they pray, but it is not obligatory.

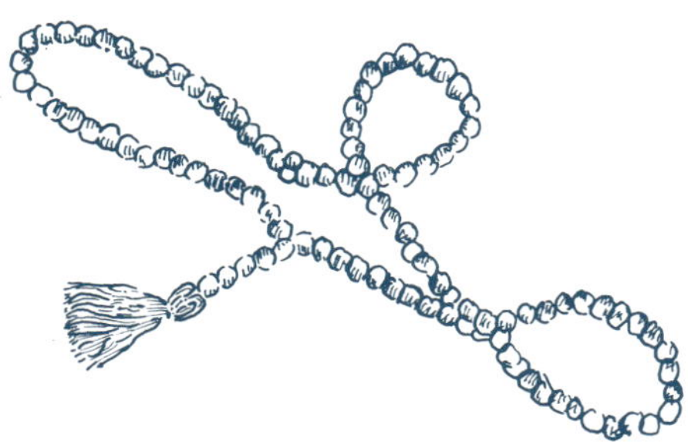

Subha / Misbaha / Tasbih

Some Muslims memorise and recite the 99 'Beautiful Names' of Allah (see page 57), counting them off on a string of 99 beads. The beads, which are sometimes arranged in three groups of 33, can be made of a variety of materials, including wood, plastic and bone. The beads are called Subha, Misbaha or Tasbih, although Tasbih really refers to the action of using the beads.

SYMBOLS

CRESCENT MOON AND STAR

One reason for the crescent moon being the symbol of Islam is that the new moon has an important influence on the Muslim way of life. The months of the Muslim calendar last from one new moon to the next. The new moon at the end of Ramadan is awaited with particular eagerness, because it signifies the end of the month of fasting and the start of the festival of Id-ul-Fitr.

It must also be remembered that in the hot desert countries of the Muslim world, the moon and stars give light and guidance to people travelling in the cool of the night. In the same way, Islam gives light and guidance to Muslims.

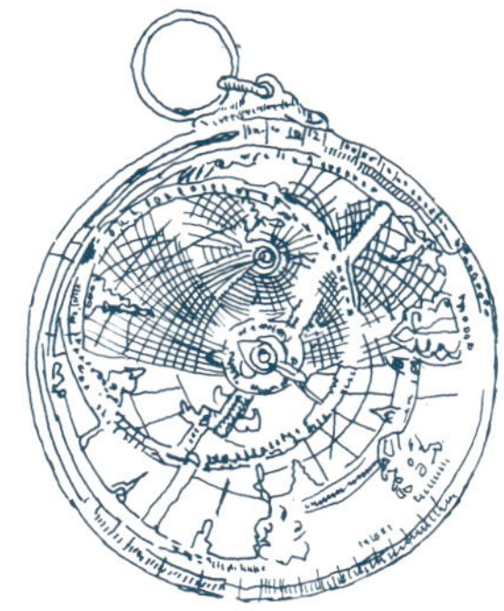

Above: *The astrolabe, used to measure the height of the stars by early navigators, was invented by Muslims.*

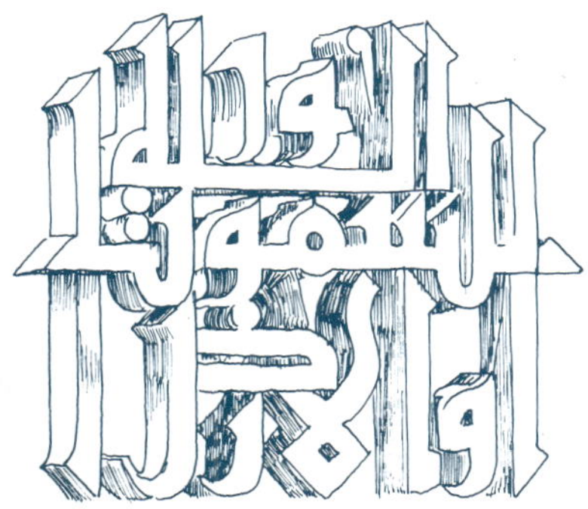

Above: *Arabic calligraphy, words taken from the Qur'an presented as a three dimensional sculpture.*

Above: *The sun which lights the day is the symbol of the Spirit which lights the next day; from a purse, Iran 20th century.*
Below: *The lion symbolises action as opposed to contemplation, for it symbolises gold and the sun, the active, directive, creative principle within all things; from a Qalamkar cloth, Iran 20th century.*

Right: *Paradise, from Humay and Humayun from poems by Khwaju Kirmani 1393* CE.

Judaism

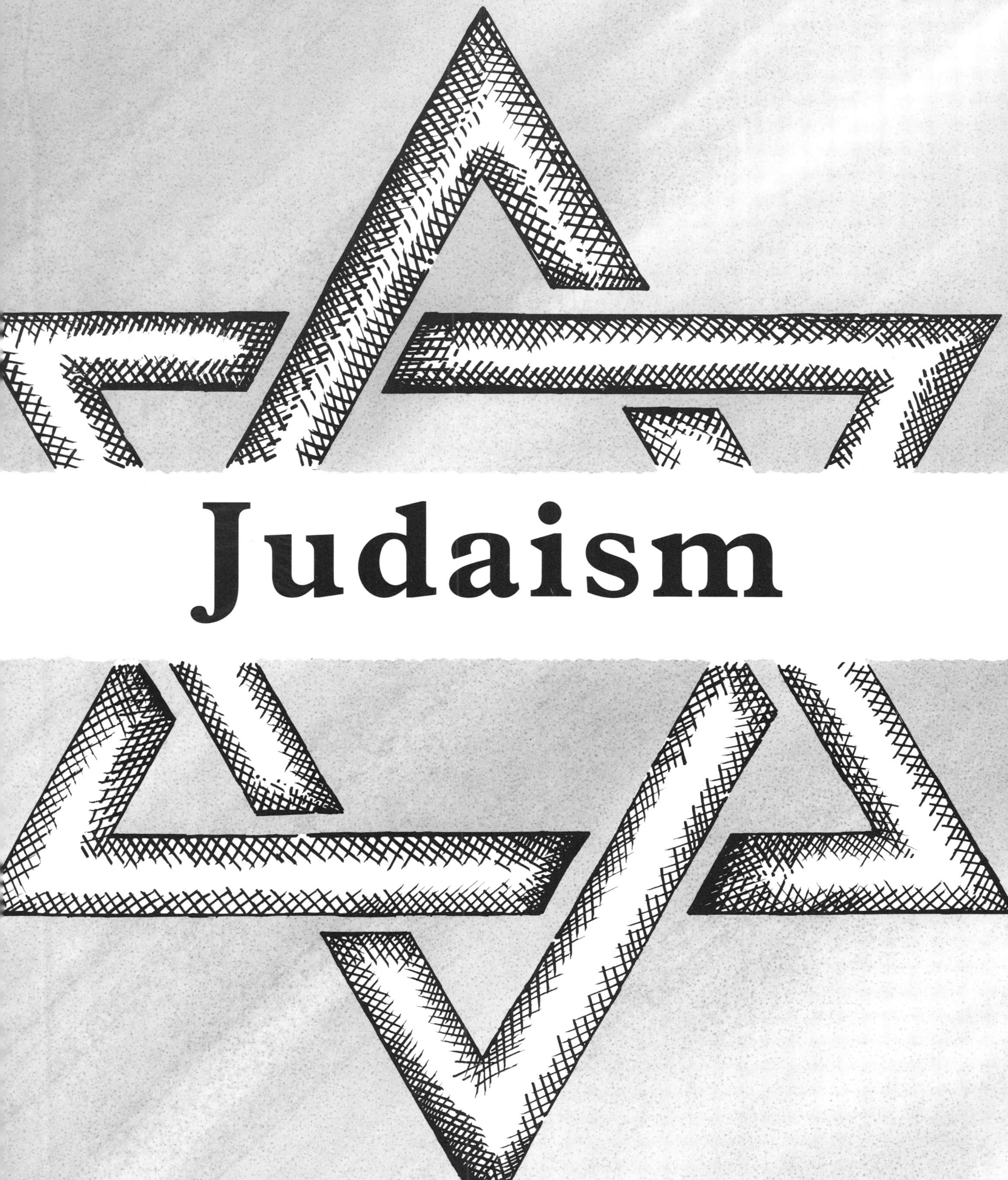

HEAR O ISRAEL: THE LORD OUR GOD IS ONE LORD;
and you shall love the Lord your God
with all your heart,
and with all your soul,
and with all your might.
And these words which I command you this day
shall be upon your heart,
and you shall teach them diligently to your children,
and shall talk of them when you sit in your house,
and when you walk by the way,
and when you lie down, and when you rise.

Deuteronomy 6. 4–7

BACKGROUND INFORMATION

THE PATRIARCHS

Abraham, the forefather of the Jewish people, lived about 4,000 years ago. He lived originally in the city of Ur which lay in the 'cradle of civilisation', the land at the mouth of the rivers Tigris and Euphrates in present-day Iraq. Abraham became a nomad, travelling to Canaan, which approximates to modern-day Israel. There God spoke to him:
'*I will give you many descendants, and some of them will be kings. You will have so many descendants that they will become nations. I will keep my promise to you and to your descendants in future generations as an everlasting covenant. I will be your God and the God of your descendants. I will give to you and to your descendants this land in which you are now a foreigner. The whole land of Canaan will belong to your descendants forever, and I will be their God.*'
(Genesis 17.6-8)
So Abraham entered into a Covenant or 'Brit' (special agreement) with God: if Abraham's descendants (the Jewish people) remained faithful to God and obeyed his laws, then God would look upon them as his special people and would take special care of them.

God renewed this Covenant with Isaac, Abraham's son, and with Jacob, Abraham's grandson. God changed Jacob's name to Israel. He had twelve sons from whom the Twelve Tribes of Israel (the Jewish people) are descended.

JEWISH HISTORY

The Covenant between God and his people was affirmed and supported by the revelation of the Torah (the first five books of the Tenakh) to Moses on Mount Sinai. This happened in about 1300 BCE, after Moses had led the Israelites out of slavery in Egypt.

After the death of Moses, Joshua led the Israelites back into Canaan, which they had to re-conquer. The land was then divided among the Twelve Tribes.

In 1030 BCE, Saul became king. He was succeeded by David, who in turn was succeeded by Solomon. Solomon built a magnificent temple in Jerusalem, in which was housed the Ark of the Covenant containing two stone slabs inscribed with the Ten Commandments.

Two kingdoms eventually developed: the Northern Kingdom of Israel and the Southern Kingdom of Judah, with Jerusalem as its capital. Both Kingdoms suffered waves of invasions by foreign armies, but the Temple remained a focus for worship until it was destroyed by the Babylonians in 586 BCE.

After the Babylonian invasion, many Jews were exiled to Babylon. Some of their descendants later returned to Jerusalem and rebuilt the Temple, but it was finally destroyed by the Romans in 70 CE. In the exile which followed, Jews settled all over the world. Today there are Jewish communities in many countries. Jewish communities outside Israel are collectively known as the Diaspora.

ORIGINS

Judaism is the oldest of the three great monotheistic religions of the Middle East, and it had a formative influence on both Christianity and Islam. People who have influenced the development of Judaism include the Patriarchs (Abraham, Isaac and Jacob) and the Prophets (such as Moses and Isaiah). The ancient history of the Jewish people is recounted in the Tenakh (*the Jewish Bible*), which contains the same material as the Old Testament in the Christian Bible.

Above: *Moses holds the Ten Commandments, written on two stone tablets.*

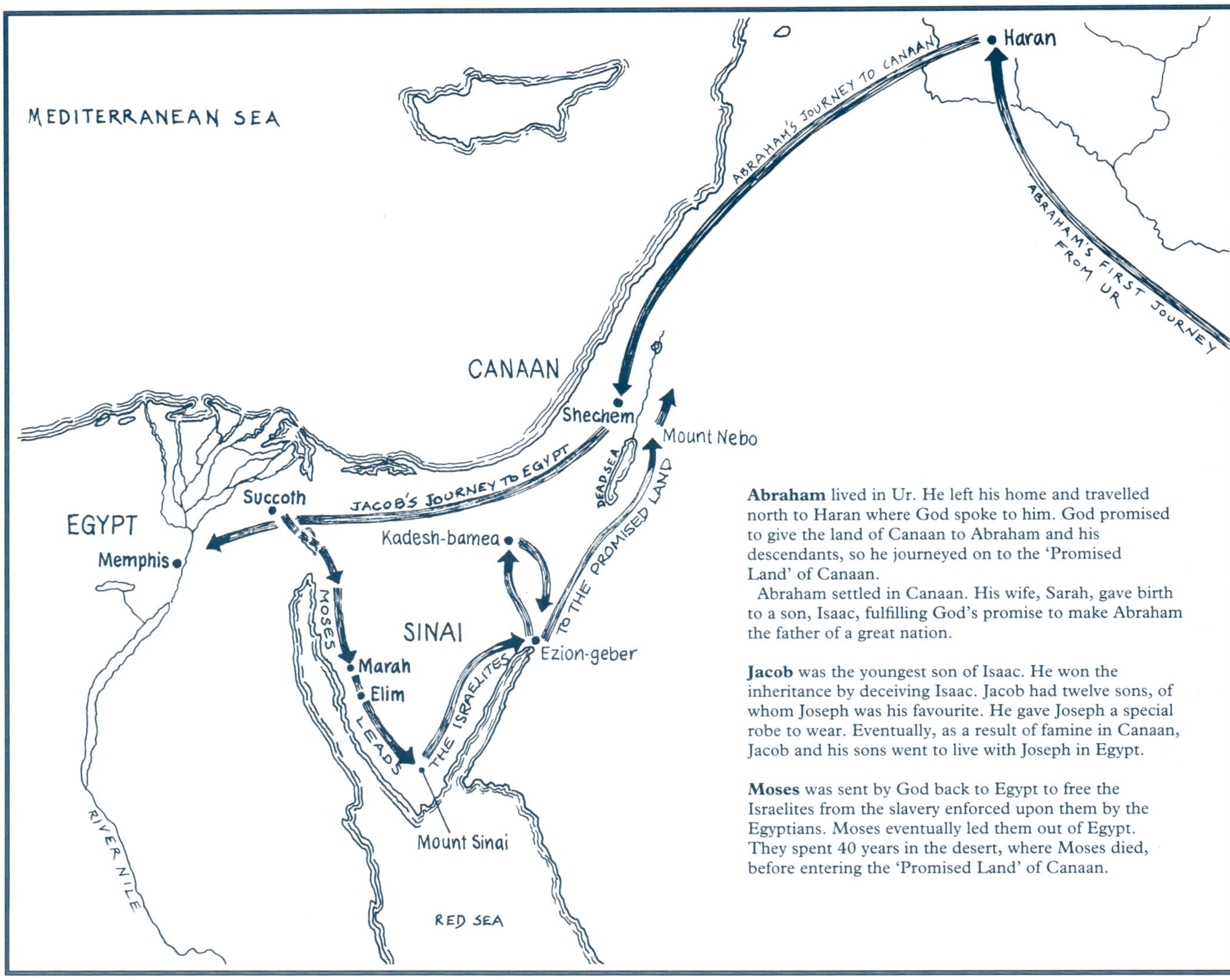

Abraham lived in Ur. He left his home and travelled north to Haran where God spoke to him. God promised to give the land of Canaan to Abraham and his descendants, so he journeyed on to the 'Promised Land' of Canaan.

Abraham settled in Canaan. His wife, Sarah, gave birth to a son, Isaac, fulfilling God's promise to make Abraham the father of a great nation.

Jacob was the youngest son of Isaac. He won the inheritance by deceiving Isaac. Jacob had twelve sons, of whom Joseph was his favourite. He gave Joseph a special robe to wear. Eventually, as a result of famine in Canaan, Jacob and his sons went to live with Joseph in Egypt.

Moses was sent by God back to Egypt to free the Israelites from the slavery enforced upon them by the Egyptians. Moses eventually led them out of Egypt. They spent 40 years in the desert, where Moses died, before entering the 'Promised Land' of Canaan.

Above: *Journeys made by Abraham, Jacob and Moses.*

The persecution inflicted upon groups of Jews down the centuries includes the Nazi Holocaust, as a result of which over six million European Jews were murdered. This was out of a worldwide Jewish population of 18 million. Partly in response to the Holocaust, the State of Israel was founded in 1948.

JEWS TODAY

There are approximately 15 million Jews worldwide. About 30% of Jews live in the USA and about 25% in Israel. Britain has a Jewish population of about 300,000, comprising both Sephardim (originally from Spain and Portugal) and Ashkenazim (originally from Central and East Europe). About 75% of practising British Jews belong to the Orthodox tradition and about 25% to the Reform and Liberal traditions.

BELIEFS AND WAY OF LIFE

GOD

The great statement of Jewish faith is the Shema, a prayer which is recited twice daily. The Shema begins with these words:

'Hear O Israel, the Lord our God is one.
And you shall love the Lord thy God with all thy heart
and with all thy soul and with all thy might'
(Deuteronomy 6.4-6)

The central belief of Judaism is that there is only one God: the creator and ruler of the whole universe. God is eternal, all-knowing and all-seeing. He is awe-inspiring in his transcendence, and yet intimately involved in the world and in the fortunes of the Jewish people.

The concept of Shekinah (*dwelling* or *residence*) is used to describe the special presence that God has with his own people, the Jews.

Above: *The Prophet Isaiah, who identified the Messiah as a suffering servant.*
Below: *Moses holds the Ten Commandments aloft.*

THE MESSIAH AND THE KINGDOM OF GOD

For thousands of years, Jews have looked forward to the arrival of the Messiah or 'Mashiach' (*Anointed One*) and the coming of the Kingdom of God. The traditional belief is that when the Messiah appears, Jews from all over the world will return to Israel where the Temple will be rebuilt for all time. The arrival of the Messiah will herald the establishment of God's Kingdom on earth, when the dead will be resurrected and '*the wolf shall dwell with the lamb*' (Isaiah 11.6)

TORAH AND MITZVOT

The Torah (*Law* or *Teaching*) is the name given to the first five books of the Tenakh (the Jewish Bible). The Torah contains 613 Mitzvot (*commandments*) covering every aspect of daily life, from civil law to personal hygiene and diet. Although many Jews no longer adhere rigidly to all 613 Mitzvot, the Ultra Orthodox try to follow them in every detail. The ten most important Mitzvot are commonly called the Ten Commandments. This set of rules forms the basis of many of the world's legal codes.

KASHRUT

Jewish dietary laws are known as Kashrut. Food that is permitted to be eaten is called Kosher (*fit* or *proper*), and anything that is not allowed is called Treife. Kosher meat must come from a herbivorous animal which chews the cud and which has cloven hooves. Beef, lamb and goat are therefore permitted, but pig is not. Poultry and fish with fins and scales are Kosher, but birds of prey, eels, octopus, squid and shellfish are all Treife. In order to be Kosher, the animal must be slaughtered in accordance with Shechita, traditional laws laid down in the Torah.

Another important aspect of Kashrut is that meat and dairy products must be kept completely separate from each other. Different utensils are used for each, and in some Jewish homes there are two sinks, two fridges, etc. Some foods, called Parve, can be eaten with either meat or milk, but generally meat cannot be eaten within three hours of the consumption of milk. Fish, fruit and vegetables are all Parve.

THE HOME

The home is regarded as the focal point of Jewish religious life. Shabbat (the weekly *Sabbath*) and many Jewish festivals are centred on the home and the family. Women, especially mothers, have an important role to play. They are responsible for safeguarding the religious purity of the home and for educating children in the ways of God.

SHABBAT (see also page 87)

***Below:** Lighting the Shabbat candles.*
***Bottom:** The Havdalah candle.*

Shabbat (*Sabbath*) is the central institution of Judaism and the most important event in Jewish life. It lasts from sunset on Friday to sunset on Saturday. It is a weekly time set aside for the family to worship, to discuss and to reflect upon Jewish teaching, and to be at leisure together.

Traditionally, certain activities and forms of work are forbidden on Shabbat, including travelling, lighting fires, preparing food, making clothes, writing, building and carrying things in public places. Orthodox Jews feel that strict adherence to these restrictions is actually a liberating experience, giving them time to concentrate on the essential features of Shabbat.

In preparation for Shabbat, all housework and preparation of food is done beforehand. The best crockery and the finest table linen are brought out for the most important family meal of the week. The family bathes and dresses in clean clothes ready to usher in this 'queen of days'. Just before the sun sets (the lighting of fire is forbidden during Shabbat) it is traditional for the mother to light two candles and to recite this blessing:

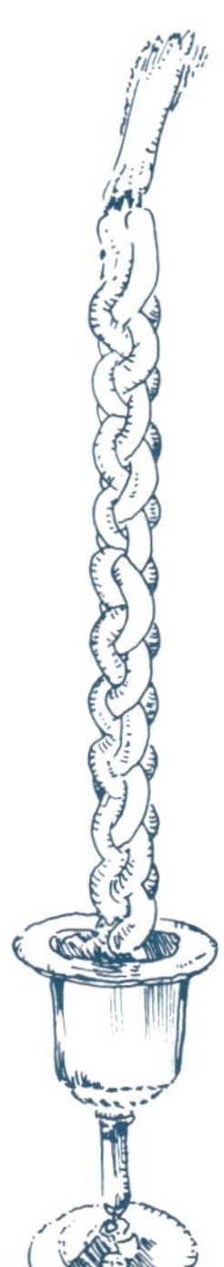

'*You are our light, O Lord, and our salvation. In your name we kindle these Sabbath lights. May they bring into our household the beauty of truth and the radiance of love's understanding*'.

When those who have been to the Synagogue have returned, the family gathers together for the Shabbat meal. The meal is preceded by a three-fold blessing called Kiddush (*holy*), which is traditionally performed by the father. First he pours wine into the Kiddush cup and blesses God, then he blesses the Shabbat day itself, and finally he blesses his wife and children. After this, at the start of the meal, two plaited loaves of bread called Challah are blessed, broken and distributed.

On the Saturday morning, the main Synagogue service of the week takes place (see page 85). On the Saturday evening, the family gathers together to bid farewell to Shabbat at a ceremony called Havdalah (*distinction*). A plaited candle with several wicks is lit, wine is sipped from a goblet filled to overflowing and everyone sniffs deeply from a spice-box, so as to take away with them the sweetness of Shabbat.

WRITINGS

THE TENAKH

The Tenakh is the Jewish Bible, written in Hebrew. The contents of the Tenakh correspond to the contents of the Old Testament in the Christian Bible, but the books are arranged in a different order. The TeNaKh comprises three sections: Torah (*Law* or *Teaching*), Nevi'im (*Prophets*) and Ketuvim (*Writings*).

Above: The title page of Genesis, from an ancient Tenakh.
Below: Reading the Torah scroll with the Yad.

THE TORAH

The most important part of the Tenakh is the Torah, which consists of the first five books: Genesis, Exodus, Leviticus, Numbers and Deuteronomy. These books are also known as the Pentateuch or the Five Books of Moses (the Torah is believed to have been revealed to Moses on Mount Sinai).

At the front of every Synagogue is the Aron Hakodesh (*Holy Ark*), a cupboard containing the Torah scrolls. During Synagogue services, the Sefer Torah (the Torah scroll–see page 86) is carried in procession to the Bimah (*dais*), the desk or platform from which it is read. As the the scroll is carried past, worshippers will touch it with the fringes of their Tallitot (*prayer shawls*) as a mark of respect. It is a great honour to be called upon to carry the Sefer Torah, to read it or to witness it being read. The reader protects the parchment by using a silver pointer called a Yad (*hand*) to keep his or her place in the text (see page 86).

Weekly readings of the Torah take place throughout the year. The festival of Simchat Torah (when the scrolls are paraded at least seven times around the Synagogue) marks the end of one annual cycle of readings and the beginning of the next (see page 77).

Every Sefer Torah is hand-copied onto parchment by a Sofer (*scribe*) who uses a goose quill. It is written out as a continuous piece of text, devoid of headings, punctuation or vowel signs. When a Sefer Torah becomes too worn to be used, it is buried in a Jewish cemetery just as a person would be buried.

NEVI'IM

Nevi'im, the second part of the Tenakh, comprises eight books: four of history and four of prophecy. The books of Joshua, Judges, Samuel and Kings tell of how God dealt with his people as they became established in Canaan, the Promised Land. The remaining four books include those of the major Prophets, Isaiah, Jeremiah and Ezekiel, and one which covers the remaining twelve Prophets.

Top: *King David, writer of some of the Psalms, playing the harp.*
Middle: *Blowing the Shofar at Rosh Hashanah.*
Bottom: *Abraham prepares to sacrifice Isaac, his son.*

KETUVIM

Ketuvim contains the remaining eleven books of the Tenakh: Psalms, Proverbs, Job, the Song of Songs, Ruth, Lamentations, Ecclesiastes, Esther, Daniel, Ezra and Nehemiah (in one book), and Chronicles.

THE TALMUD

In about 200 CE, a large oral tradition of judgements and opinions developed over hundreds of years was formalised and collected together in a document called the Mishnah. The Mishnah itself then became the subject of scholarly debate and reinterpretation, as a result of which a commentary called the Gemara was produced. The Mishnah and the Gemara were eventually combined in the Talmud, a huge volume that has a profound influence on the way that Jews live out their beliefs.

FESTIVALS

ROSH HASHANAH (September)

Rosh Hashanah (*Head of the Year*), is the Jewish New Year. It celebrates the creation of the world, but it is also a time to review the past year, to reflect and to pray. Rosh Hashanah is also called the Day of Judgement. The Shofar (ram's horn – see page 87) is blown in the Synagogue as a reminder of Abraham's sacrifice of a ram instead of Isaac, his son. Sweet foods are eaten, including apples dipped in honey, symbolising the hope that the year ahead will be sweet.

YOM KIPPUR (September/October)

Yom Kippur (*Day of Atonement*) comes ten days after Rosh Hashanah. It is the most solemn and serious day of the year. Almost the whole day is spent at the Synagogue in prayer, reflection and repentance, and for 24 hours neither food nor water may be taken. In the days leading up to Yom Kippur, Jews are expected to do everything they can to settle grievances. As they seek forgiveness from those they have wronged, so they seek forgiveness from God.

SUKKOT (September/October)

Sukkot is an autumn harvest festival which reminds Jews of the 40 years spent in the wilderness after Moses had led their ancestors out of Egypt. As they wandered through the desert, the Israelites lived in makeshift shelters or 'Sukkot' (*booths, huts* or *tabernacles*). Similar shelters were used at harvest time.

During the festival, which lasts for over a week, some Jewish families erect Sukkot in their gardens. A Sukkah is generally a cube-shaped structure with a flat roof decorated with branches and hanging fruits. Families eat in them and sometimes sleep in them.

The Arba Minim (*four species*) are four types of plant associated with Sukkot. Their shapes are reminiscent of different parts of the body: the Lulav (*date palm*) corresponds to the spine; the Etrog (*citron*) corresponds to the heart; the Haddassim (*myrtle leaves*) correspond to the eyes; the Aravot (*willow branches*) correspond to the lips. All of these

Above: *A family inside a Sukkah.*
Right: *A Sukkah.*

should be united in worship of God, and to symbolise this the Etrog is held in the left hand while the other three plants are bound together and held in the right hand. On every day of the festival, the four plants are shaken three times in every direction: to the east, south, west and north.

Above: *The four species; the Lulav (date palm), Etrog (citron), Haddassim (myrtle leaves) and Aravah (willow branch).*
Below: *A modern Hanukiah ready for the second night of the Hanukkah festival. The Shamash (servant candle) is on the right.*

SIMCHAT TORAH (October)

Simchat Torah (*Rejoicing of the Law*) celebrates the completion of the annual cycle of readings from the Torah and the beginning of a new cycle of readings. The Torah scrolls are carried at least seven times around the Synagogue, followed by children singing, dancing and waving flags. The children are given sweets.

HANUKKAH (December)

Hanukkah celebrates the Jewish victory over the Greek-Syrians and the subsequent re-dedication of the Temple (see story on page 78). During the eight nights of the festival candles are lit: one on the first night, two on the second and so on until the eighth night. Each night the candles burn right down to be replaced the following night. The candles are placed in a special nine-branched candlestick, technically called a Hanukiah (see page 87) but widely known as a Hanukkah Menorah. During Hanukkah children play a traditional game with a spinning top called a Dreidel (see page 87), and foods cooked in oil, such as doughnuts and latkes (potato pancakes), are eaten.

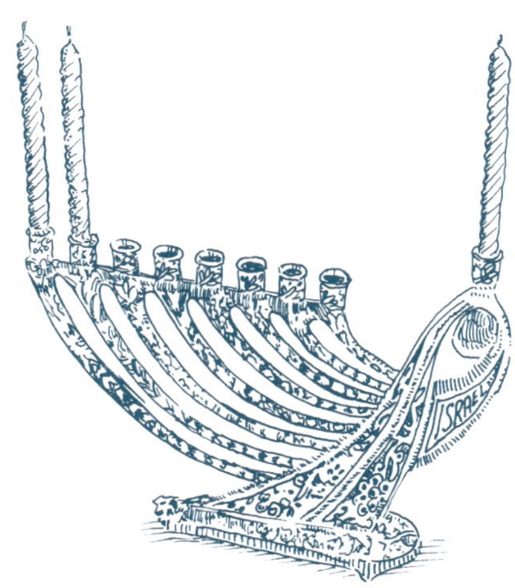

The story behind Hanukkah

The land that is today called Israel once comprised part of the Syrian Empire. In 168 BCE the Syrian emperor, Antiochus IV, who was Greek, decided to impose Greek culture throughout his empire. His army invaded Jerusalem, pigs were sacrificed on the high altar of the Temple and a statue of Zeus was erected in the Holy of Holies. Jews were forced to eat pork and to perform sacrifices both to Greek gods and to Antiochus himself.

Then a Jewish revolt broke out. A small band of Jewish fighters, led first by a priest called Mattathias and later by Judah the Maccabee, his son, used guerilla tactics to defeat the army of Antiochus. In 165 BCE Judah the Maccabee entered the Temple and re-dedicated it to the God of the Jews. He found a small jar of oil, just enough to keep the great Menorah (seven-branched candelabrum) alight for one day. But when the Menorah lamps were lit, the oil continued to burn for eight days until fresh supplies arrived. The festival of Hanukkah celebrates this miracle.

TU BI-SHVAT (February)

Tu bi-Shvat (New Year for Trees) is an ancient festival during which trees are planted. Today it provides an opportunity for Jews to celebrate the remarkable transformation of Israel from a largely barren wasteland into a green and fertile land. Jews living in Israel celebrate by going on picnics. Jews living outside Israel celebrate by eating fruit grown in Israel.

PURIM (February/March)

Purim is a joyous festival dating from the fifth century BCE. During the festival, Jews recall how Esther, the Jewish wife of a Persian king, bravely saved her people by foiling prime minister Haman's plot (see story on page 79).

The story is read in the Synagogue from a special scroll called the Megillat Esther (see page 88). Whenever Haman's name is mentioned, a tremendous din ensues. There are boos and cat-calls, feet are stamped, trumpets are blown, drums are beaten, and greggers, resembling rattles used by football supporters, are whirled (see page 88). Whenever Esther's name is mentioned, everyone cheers!

The festival is characterised by much feasting and drinking. The food most closely associated with Purim is the three-cornered pastry usually filled with poppy-seed and honey called Hamantaschen (Haman's pockets) in Yiddish or German. In Israel the pastries are called Oznoi Haman (Haman's ears).There are also fancy dress parades and a carnival queen, dressed as Esther, is chosen.

Above: *The Megillat Esther.*
Right: *Children wearing fancy dress for the festival of Purim.*

The story behind Purim

About 2,500 years ago, the great Persian Empire was ruled over by King Ahasuerus. A beautiful Jewish woman called Esther became his queen. Esther's parents had died when she was young and she had been brought up by her older cousin, Mordecai. The king didn't know that she was Jewish, or that Mordecai, who was one of his administrators, was her cousin.

One day Mordecai discovered that two servants were plotting to kill the king. He told Esther, who warned her husband. The two men were executed, and Mordecai's good deed was noted in the official records.

Some time later, the king made Haman his prime minister. Everyone was required to bow down before Haman, but Mordecai refused to do so. When questioned about his behaviour, he explained that he was a Jew and that he would bow only before God. This made Haman very angry, and he vowed to find a way to kill not only Mordecai, but all the Jews in the Persian Empire. He decided that all Jews would be killed eleven months later, on the thirteenth day of the twelfth month. Haman arrived at this day by casting lots (Purim means lots).

Haman went to the King and told him that there were people in the Empire who refused to obey his laws. If the king would issue a decree ordering these rebels to be put to death, Haman would fill the king's coffers with silver. The king obliged, and the decree was made known throughout the Empire. All Jews, young and old, men, women and children were to be killed.

When Mordecai heard what had happened, he sent Esther a message begging her to speak to the king. Although Esther was King Ahasuerus' wife, she was bound by the same laws as any of his subjects. No one could approach the king without being summoned by him: the penalty for doing so was death.

Esther asked all the Jews to fast for three days, and then she put on her finest robes and bravely stood outside the throne room in full view of her husband. When the king saw her, he was so struck by her beauty that he held out his gold sceptre for her to touch and offered her anything she wanted, up to half his empire. She replied that all she wanted was for her husband and Haman to dine with her.

That night, the king could not sleep. In his restless state, he listened to the official state records being read and he was reminded of how Mordecai had saved him. He sent for Haman, and asked him: '*What should be done for a man whom the king wants to honour?*'

Thinking that Ahasuerus had him in mind, Haman replied that he should be led through the streets in a royal robe on a royal horse. To Haman's surprise, the king ordered Haman to bestow this honour upon Mordecai. Haman had no choice but to lead Mordecai through the streets proclaiming: '*See how the king rewards a man he wishes to honour!*'

That night, at Esther's private banquet for the king and Haman, she told her husband that an evil man was plotting to murder all her people. When the king asked her to identify the man, she told him that it was Haman. Ahasuerus then ordered Haman to be hanged on the very gallows that he had erected for Mordecai.

The king now learned that Esther was a Jew and that Mordecai was her cousin. He made Mordecai his senior adviser. All the Jews were saved and there were great celebrations. These celebrations are recalled every year during the festival of Purim.

PESACH (March/April)

Pesach (*Passover*) celebrates the spring barley harvest, but the festival is mainly concerned with remembering how Moses led the Israelites out of slavery in Egypt to freedom (see story on page 81). Before Pesach begins, houses are thoroughly cleaned. Throughout the eight-day festival, food and drink made with leaven are not eaten or drunk. Matzot (see page 88) are substituted for bread, and traditional homes are emptied of all food and drink made with leaven: bread, cakes, biscuits, pasta, beer, whisky, etc.

Top: *A box of Matzot.*
Above: *A Matzot cover depicting a Seder plate.*
Below: *A Seder plate.*

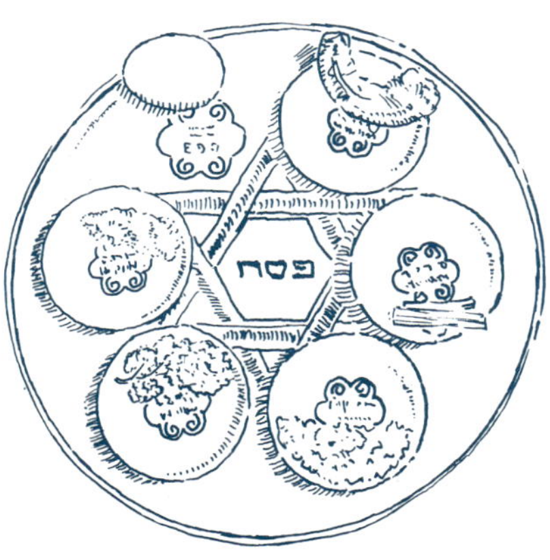

The Seder Service (see also page 88)
On the first two evenings of Pesach, families hold a Seder service at home, during which a celebratory meal is eaten. Seder means 'order', and to guide the family through the service, everyone present has a Hagadah (*telling*), a book which re-tells the story of the Exodus and which describes the various rituals which are performed to re-create the dramatic events of the story.

For the service, the family sits around the dinner table. In the centre of the table are three Matzot, slotted into a special cover, and the Seder plate, divided into various sections for the different foods that are placed upon it. Each item of food has a symbolic meaning relating to the Exodus story:

Three Matzot (thin wafers of unleavened bread): a reminder of the fact that the Israelites left Egypt in too great a hurry to be able to bake their bread with leaven. (The middle Matzah is broken in two. One half, called the Afikomen (*dessert*), is hidden and the children have to find it during the meal which follows the Seder service.)

A roasted shankbone of lamb (not eaten): a reminder of the lambs that were sacrificed and the blood that was smeared on the doors of the Israelite homes to protect them from the Angel of Death.

A roasted egg (not eaten): a symbol of the new life that awaited the Israelites in the Promised Land.

Karpas (a leafy vegetable such as parsley): a reminder of spring, but before it is eaten it is dipped in salt water as a reminder of the tears and sweat of the slaves.

Maror (a bitter herb such as horseradish): a reminder of the bitterness of slavery.

Haroset (a sticky paste made of grated apples, cinnamon, chopped nuts, honey and wine): a reminder of the mortar used by the slaves on Pharaoh's building projects, and also of the sweetness of freedom.

During the Seder service, four glasses of wine are drunk, each one serving as a reminder of a promise made by God to the Israelites:
'I shall liberate you from bondage'
'I shall bring you to the land'
'I shall deliver you from Egypt'
'I shall take you to me as a people'.

As a result of a fifth promise, '*I shall redeem you from servitude*', a cup of wine is filled for the prophet Elijah. This cup is not drunk. At the end of the meal, the door is opened to allow Elijah to enter. His arrival will usher in a time of eternal freedom for the Jewish people.

At one point in the service, the names of the ten plagues which God inflicted on the Egyptians are recited. As each plague is mentioned, a drop of wine is spilt.

The youngest child present has a special function to perform. After enquiring '*Why is this night different from all other nights?*', he or she asks the four questions: '*Why do we have unleavened bread?*'; *Why do we eat bitter herbs?*'; '*Why do we dip our herbs in salt water?*'; '*Why do we sit in a reclining position on cushions?*'.

The Seder service and the family meal which follows are interspersed with songs about the escape from Egypt and anecdotal stories. The Seder ends with the cry: '*Next year in Jerusalem!*'; or, in Israel: '*Next year in Jerusalem rebuilt!*'.

The story behind Pesach

Long before the time of Jesus, the Israelites, who were the ancestors of the Jews, lived in Egypt. They were treated as slaves by the Pharaoh. They longed to be free and to return to their homeland.

One day Pharaoh's daughter rescued a baby boy from the reeds that grew by the River Nile. Pharaoh had ordered all Israelite baby boys to be killed. One mother had placed her baby in a basket and had hidden it in the reeds. Pharaoh's daughter did not realise that the baby was an Israelite, and the boy was brought up in the royal palace. He was given an Egyptian name, Moses, but he knew that he was really an Israelite.

Years later God appeared to Moses in a burning bush in the desert. God told Moses to lead the Israelites from slavery to freedom. Moses went with his brother Aaron to the court of the Pharaoh and asked him to let the slaves go. Pharaoh refused. Again and again Moses pleaded with the Pharaoh. Each time he refused, God sent a plague on the land.

There were ten plagues: the River Nile turned red with blood; there were swarms of frogs, gnats and flies; a disease killed all the cattle; the Egyptians suffered from boils; there were thunderstorms and hailstones; locusts ate all the leaves and grass; and darkness covered the land for three days. During the final plague the Angel of Death passed over, killing the first-born children of the Egyptians. The Israelites protected their homes by smearing lambs' blood on their doorposts.

This final plague resulted in the death of Pharaoh's own son, and now he begged the slaves to leave. The Israelites decided to go quickly before the Egyptians changed their minds. They gathered their belongings together, and because there was no time to make bread with yeast, they ate unleavened bread instead.

Moses led the slaves to the edge of the Red Sea, but now they saw dust clouds behind them. Pharaoh's grief had turned to anger, and he had sent soldiers in chariots to pursue the slaves. Moses stretched his hand out, and the waters of the Red Sea miraculously parted. The Israelites made their way to safety, but the Egyptian soldiers who tried to follow became stuck in the mud and were drowned. The slaves were free at last.

Above: *Emblem of the State of Israel.*

YOM HA-SHOAH (April)

Yom ha-Shoah (*Day of Desolation*) is a day of remembrance for the victims of the Nazi Holocaust. Memorial candles are lit, and Synagogue services include readings and poems from books written about the Holocaust.

YOM HA-ATZMAUT (April/May)

Yom ha-Atzmaut (*Independence Day*) is a modern festival celebrating the creation of the State of Israel in 1948. Its instigation follows the Jewish tradition of imbuing historically significant events with religious significance. The celebrations include parties, the singing of Israeli songs and dancing.

SHAVUOT (May/June)

Shavuot (*weeks*), also known as the Feast of Weeks or Pentecost, takes place seven weeks after Pesach. It recalls the giving of the Torah to Moses on Mount Sinai, and it celebrates the summer wheat harvest. The story of Ruth, with its harvest theme (see below) is read out in Synagogues. For Shavuot, Synagogues are decorated with flowers, and dairy foods such as cheesecake and blintzes (pancakes filled with cream cheese) are eaten.

A story associated with Shavuot

Long ago there was a terrible famine in the land of Israel. A man called Elimelech left Bethlehem and settled in the country of Moab with Naomi, his wife, and his two sons. The sons grew up and married Moabite women. Elimelech died, and so did his two sons. This left Naomi alone with her two Moabite daughters-in-law.

Naomi decided to return to Israel. One of her daughters-in-law remained in Moab; the other, Ruth, persuaded Naomi to let her accompany her back to Israel. They arrived back in Bethlehem during the barley harvest. Ruth joined the other gleaners, gathering up the small amount of grain that had been left on the ground after the labourers had harvested the crop.

A man called Boaz, who was the owner of the field in which Ruth was working, enquired about her. Although she was a foreigner, he allowed her to carry on gleaning and he treated her as though she was an Israelite. He recognised the devotion and loyalty that she had displayed towards Naomi, and when Ruth showed him similar kindness, he decided to marry her.

After they were married, Ruth and Boaz had a son called Obed. Obed grew up and had a son called Jesse. Jesse grew up and had a son called David. And David grew up to be the great King of Israel.

TISHAH B'AV (July/August)

Tishah b'Av commemorates tragic events in Jewish history. It is a day of mourning and fasting, during which the Book of Lamentations is read. The day recalls the destruction of the first and second Temples in Jerusalem and other sad events, such as the expulsion of Jews from England in 1290 CE and from Spain in 1492 CE.

RITES OF PASSAGE

BIRTH

Brit Milah

When Jewish boys are eight days old, Brit Milah (*Covenant of Circumcision*) is performed. The removal of the foreskin of the penis is an ancient tradition, and one that is important in terms of Jewish identity. Brit Milah is an occasion for family celebration and as part of the ceremony the baby is named. A baby girl can be named in the Synagogue a week after she is born.

COMING OF AGE

Bar / Bat Mitzvah

When a Jewish boy reaches the age of 13, he is considered old enough to take on adult religious responsibilities. For many years he will have received instruction in Hebrew and in the Torah. On the Saturday morning of Shabbat immediately following his thirteenth birthday, he is called upon to read from the Torah scroll in the Synagogue. This honour bestows on him the title of Bar Mitzvah (*Son of the Commandment*). On this important occasion, it is likely that he will wear a Tallit (*prayer shawl*) for the first time, and be given Tefillin if he is an Orthodox Jew (see page 86). The Synagogue service is followed by a family celebration.

Communities of Reform and Liberal Jews allow girls to read from the Torah from the age of 12. A girl who does this becomes a Bat Mitzvah (*Daughter of the Commandment*), and similar celebrations are held for her.

MARRIAGE

Jewish weddings cannot take place on Shabbat or on festival days, so they are often held on Sundays. The ceremony usually takes place in the Synagogue or, in Israel, in the open air. The bride, wearing white, and the groom stand under the Huppah, a canopy supported by four poles. The Huppah is usually decorated with flowers, and it represents the home that the couple will soon share.

The Rabbi blesses a cup of wine which the couple share. The groom puts a ring on the forefinger of the bride's right hand and announces: *'Behold you are sanctified to me with this ring, according to the Law of Moses and Israel'*. The couple are now married.

The Ketubah (marriage contract) is then read out. This document will have been prepared beforehand. Traditionally, it sets out the husband's responsibilities to his wife.

Seven marriage blessings are said by the Rabbi, and the ceremony ends when the groom stamps on a wine glass to shouts of *'Mazel Tov!'* (*good luck*). The smashing of the wine glass reminds Jews of the destruction of the Temple and of the fact that even in moments of great personal happiness one should not forget the sufferings of others.

Top: *A boy reading from the Torah scroll wearing a Tallit and Tefillin.*
Above: *A bride and groom standing under the Huppah.*

DEATH

Beliefs

Jews are far more concerned with this world than with ha-Olam ha-Ba (*the World to Come*), but they believe in an afterlife in which God will judge each soul according to its actions in this life. Some strict Orthodox Jews still speak of Sheol, a shadowy underground place where the ghosts of the dead await bodily resurrection. There is a tradition that on the Last Day, the Messiah (see page 73) will appear and the dead will come back to life in their physical bodies. For this reason bodies are not cremated in traditional Jewish communities. Reform and Liberal Jews do practise cremation, but it is a traditional burial that is described below.

Customs

Jews try to die with the words of the Shema (see page 73) on their lips. The funeral takes place as soon as possible, usually the day after death, unless this is Shabbat or a festival day. The body is washed and wrapped in a white shroud and/or a Tallit (*prayer shawl*). The body must not be left unattended at any time. The main mourners sometimes make a cut in their coats, recalling the days when mourners tore their clothing.

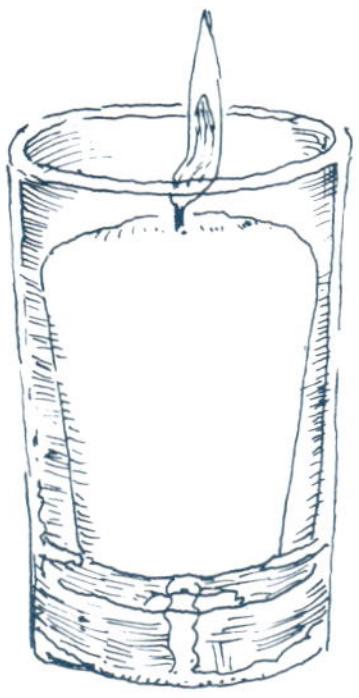

The body is buried in a Jewish cemetery while the Kaddish (a prayer proclaiming the glory of God) is read by relatives. The Kaddish is recited every day in the year of mourning and on every anniversary of the person's death. Flowers are not encouraged at funerals.

Shiva is a period of seven days of intense mourning following a funeral. During Shiva, all ordinary work is prohibited for the bereaved. Shiva is followed by Sheloshim, a month when the mourners do not go to any entertainment.

Above: *A Yahrzeit candle.*
Below: *A modern Orthodox Synagogue, a place for meeting and for worship.*

Each year, on the anniversary of the person's death, there is a ceremony called Yahrzeit. A memorial candle is lit and burnt for 24 hours. The grave may be visited. It is customary for visitors to place a stone on the grave before they leave.

PLACES OF WORSHIP

THE SYNAGOGUE

A Synagogue is essentially a meeting place: a place where members of the Jewish community can gather together for study and worship. In addition to the main room, which is used for worship, Synagogues often contain rooms for study, meetings and social functions.

The large room used for worship cannot usually be entered directly from the street, and before going in, males put on hats or head coverings. In Orthodox Synagogues, married women as well as men are expected to cover their heads.

The main feature of the Synagogue is the Aron Hakodesh (*Holy Ark*), a cupboard containing the Torah scrolls. The Aron Hakodesh is set into the wall that is nearest to Jerusalem (in Britain this would be the east wall). The Ner Tamid (*Eternal Light*) hangs above the Aron Hakodesh to symbolise the presence of God.

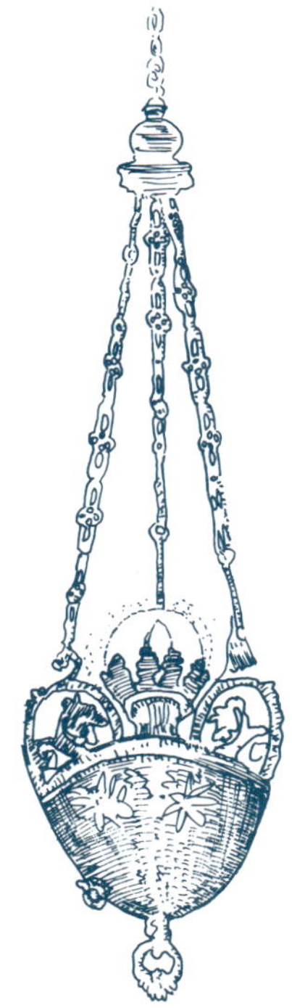

In the middle of the Synagogue is the Bimah (*dais*), a raised platform from which the Torah scrolls are read and prayers are led.

In Orthodox Synagogues there is a gallery where women and older girls sit separately from the men. Younger girls can sit with their fathers brothers. In Reform and Liberal Synagogues men, women and children sit together.

Worship at the synagogue

The main weekly act of worship takes place in the Synagogue on Saturday morning, during Shabbat. In addition to their hats or Kippot (skullcaps–see page 86), all the men, including boys who have been through the Bar Mitzvah ceremony (see page 83), wear Tallitot (*prayer shawls*).

The service consists mainly of readings from the Torah and prayers. Hebrew is used to a much greater extent in Orthodox Synagogues than in Reform and Liberal Synagogues. The prayers always include the Amidah (*standing*), which each member of the congregation says silently while standing, and the Kaddish, a prayer of sanctification.

The prayers and readings are usually led by a Rabbi or by a Cantor, a man who is trained to sing or to intone the words in the appropriate manner. The Rabbi, who is an authorised Jewish teacher, often preaches a sermon. In Reform and Liberal Synagogues, the Rabbi may be a woman.

THE WESTERN WALL

The Dome of the Rock, which is a Muslim shrine, now occupies part of the site where the Temple once stood in Jerusalem. Of the actual Temple, nothing remains. The Western Wall, which is sometimes referred to incorrectly as the wailing wall, forms one side of the huge platform which supported the Temple. This is a place of great significance for Jews. From all over the world, they come to touch and kiss the stones and to pray. The cracks between the stones are filled with pieces of paper on which prayers have been written.

Above: *The Ner Tamid (*Eternal Light*).*
Below: *Worship at the Western Wall.*

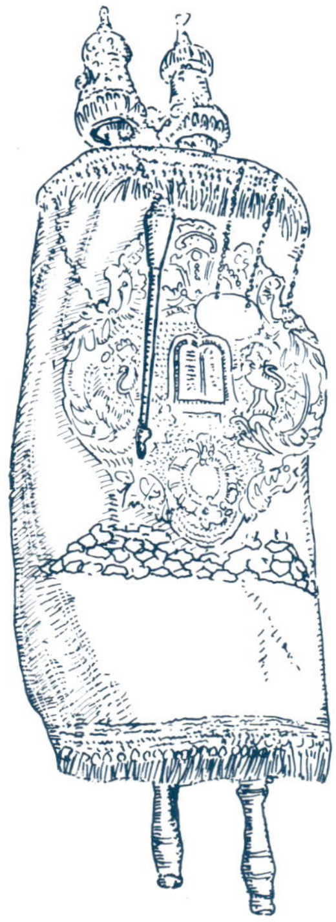

RITUAL OBJECTS AND ARTEFACTS

SCROLLS

Sefer Torah (see page 75)
The Sefer Torah (Torah scroll) is handwritten on parchment. In Ashkenazi Synagogues, the Torah scrolls are kept in embroidered cloth covers. Miniature crowns with bells attached fit over the top of two wooden rollers. Each roller is called Aytz Hayim (*Tree of Life*). A breast-plate, like the one once worn by the High Priest, is hung around the scroll. In Sephardi Synagogues, the Sefer Torah is incorporated into a wooden or metal case. Torah scrolls are sacred and are rarely seen outside the Synagogue, but smaller replicas are readily available.

Yad
The Torah scroll is too holy to be touched, so the reader keeps her/his place in the text by using a special silver pointer called a Yad. This also protects the parchment. The end of the Yad (*hand*) is in the shape of a hand with an outstretched forefinger.

Mezuzah
The Mezuzah is a miniature scroll on which the first two paragraphs of the Shema (see page 73) are written. The Shema includes the words: *And you shall write them* (the words of the Shema) *on the doorposts of your house and on your gate*. To comply with this command, the Mezuzah is placed in a small narrow container which is attached to the door frames of buildings, including some Jewish homes and Synagogues. As Ultra Orthodox Jews pass through the doorway, they touch the Mezuzah case and kiss their fingers.

CLOTHING

Kippah
The Kippah (also known as a Yamulkah or Capel) is a skullcap worn by males as a symbol of their Jewish identity. In Israel, many men wear Kippahs all the time. In Britain they are worn in the Synagogue and during religious ceremonies in the home.

Tallit
The Tallit is a shawl worn by Jewish males for prayer. To wrap oneself in a Tallit is to remind oneself that God is all around. The Tallit is white, with blue or black stripes towards each end. At each end of the Tallit there are fringes, and at each corner there are long threads called Tziziot. Each Tzizit is tied in five knots representing the five books of the Torah. Young Jewish boys often wear Tallitot, but for many the first occasion when a Tallit is worn is the Bar Mitzvah ceremony. The Tallit is often used as a burial shroud.

Tefillin
Tefillin, sometimes called Phylacteries, consist of two small black leather boxes attached to long leather straps. The boxes contain passages from the Shema (see page 86) and from Exodus 13. The Shema includes the words: *And you shall bind them* (the words of the Shema) as *a sign upon your hand, and they shall be as frontlets between your eyes*.

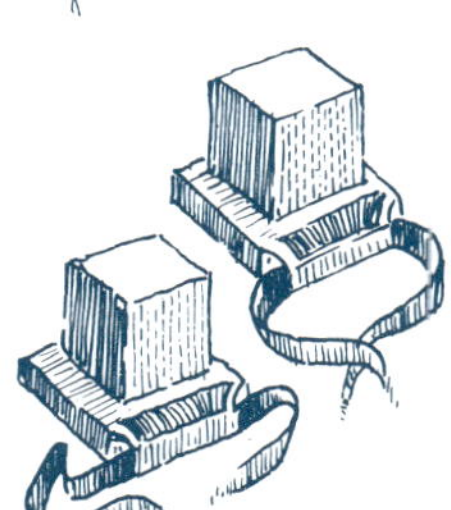

In obedience to this command, male Orthodox Jews tie Tefillin on to their left arms and foreheads for morning prayers on ordinary weekdays. They are not worn on Shabbat or on festival days. By binding Tefillin on to their upper left arms and onto their foreheads, the wearers ensure that the words of the Shema lie next to the heart, which is associated with feeling, and next to the head, which is associated with thinking.

SHABBAT (see page 74)

Candlesticks

As the sun sets at the start of Shabbat, the mother lights two candles and recites a blessing. The candlesticks used in the home are usually made of precious metal, and they may well be family heirlooms. She will also have a smaller pair, to use when the family is staying away from home.

Kiddush Cup

The Kiddush cup is filled with wine which is blessed by the father during the family ceremony which takes place at the start of Shabbat.

Challah Loaves and Cover

For the family ceremony at the start of Shabbat, two plaited loaves, called Challah, are specially baked. These are placed under an ornately embroidered cloth before being blessed, broken and distributed.

Havdalah Candle

During Havdalah, the ceremony which marks the end of Shabbat, a plaited candle with several wicks is lit. The blessing said over the candle refers to 'lights' in the plural, hence the multiple wicks. The candle is usually given to a child to hold and the flame is usually put out by being immersed in a cup of wine.

Havdalah Spice-Box

Havdalah spice-boxes vary in appearance. They may be of simple design and made of wood or highly ornate and made of silver. During the Havdalah ceremony, the spice-box is passed around so that everyone in the family can sniff the spices inside and carry the sweetness of Shabbat with them into the following week.

ROSH HASHANAH (see page 76)

Shofar

The Shofar is a ram's horn trumpet. It heralds the new year by being blown repeatedly in the Syngogue during the festival of Rosh Hashanah (see page 76). Its sound urges Jews to put past failings behind them and to look ahead to the future.

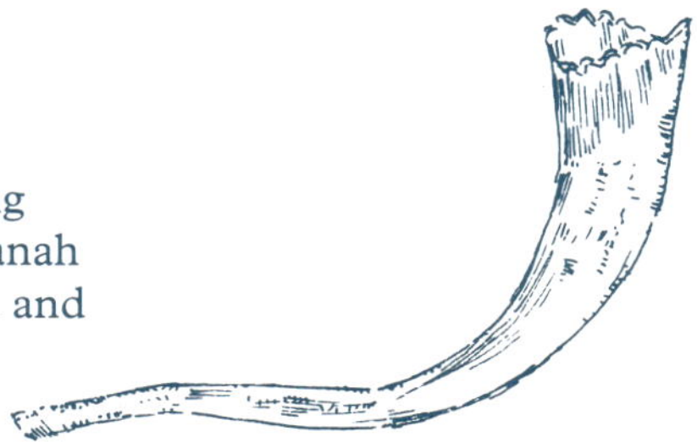

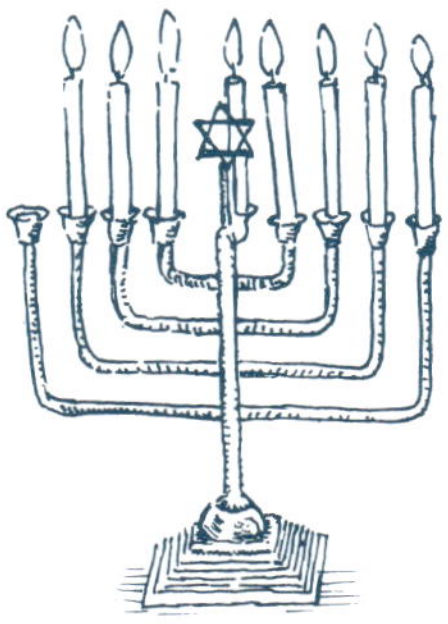

HANUKKAH (see page 77)

Hanukiah

Hanukiah is the correct name for the candlestick used during the festival of Hanukkah, although it is often referred to as the Hanukkah Menorah. The Hanukiah can be of any design so long as it holds eight candles at the same level and a ninth candle, from which the others are lit over the eight nights of the festival. The ninth candle is called the Shamash (*servant*).

Dreidel

The Dreidel is a small four-sided spinning top used by children to play a traditional game during the festival of Hanukkah. On each side of the Dreidel there is a Hebrew letter, the equivalents of 'n', 'g', 'h' and 'sh'. These are the first letters of the words in the Hebrew phrase *'Nes gadol haya sham'* (*'A great miracle happened here'*).

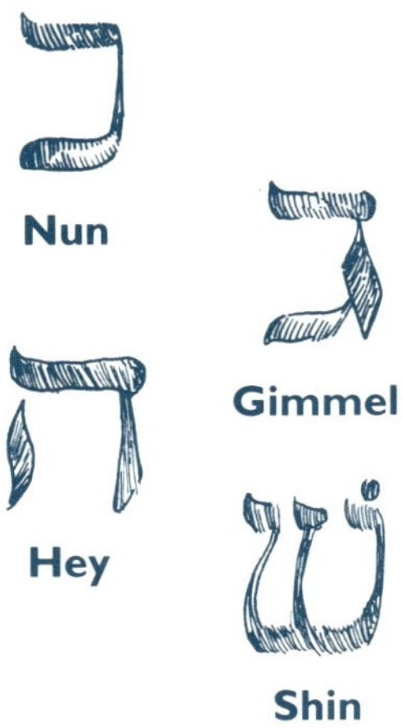

The rules of the Dreidel game are as follows:

1 Counters (nuts or sweets are often used) are divided equally among all players.
2 Each player puts one counter into kitty.
3 First player spins Dreidel and complies with instruction indicated by Hebrew letter on top:

Nun	= do nothing
Gimmel	= take all the kitty
Hey	= take half the kitty
Shin	= put a counter into kitty

4 Each player puts one counter into kitty.
5 Second player spins Dreidel, etc.

Players drop out when they have lost all their counters.
The game ends when the winner has collected all the counters.

PURIM (see page 78)

Megillat Esther

During the festival of Purim, the story of Esther is read from a special scroll called the Megillat Esther, which contains the book of Esther and which often includes illustrations of the story.

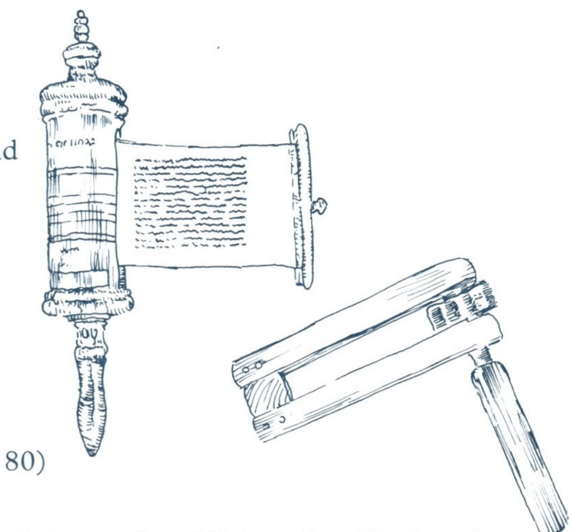

Gregger

Greggers resemble the rattles whirled by football fans, which have a characteristic 'clacking' sound. They are used during Purim to help to drown out Haman's name as the story of Esther is read out in the Syngogue.

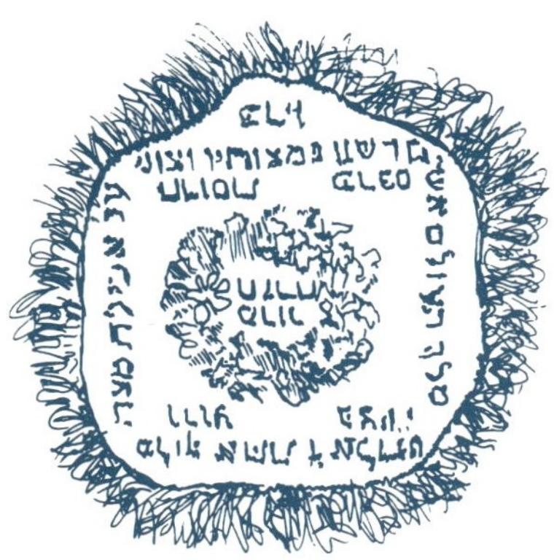

THE SEDER SERVICE (see page 80)

Matzot and Cover

A Matzah (Matzot in the plural) is a wafer of flat cracker-like bread baked before it rises. Boxes of Matzot (Rukusen's is the usual brand!) are readily available in supermarkets, especially at the time of Pesach (Passover) when bread made with yeast is prohibited (see page 80).

During the Seder service, which takes place at the start of Pesach, the story of the Exodus from Egypt is re-told (see page 81). Three Matzot are used during the service. They are slotted into three sections of an embroidered cloth cover.

Seder Plate

The Seder plate is a round plate divided into various sections which hold the symbolic foods used during the Seder service: a shankbone of lamb, a roasted egg, Karpas, Maror and Haroset (see page 80). The most valuable Seder plates are made of silver, often handed down through the family, but more usually they are made of china or a cheaper metal such as tin.

Hagadah

The Hagadah (*telling*) is the book used to re-tell the story of the Exodus at the Seder service. It also describes the varous rituals that are performed during the service. It is written in Hebrew, but there are versions available with translations. All the participants in the Seder service have their own copy. There are children's versions that are attractively illustrated.

SYMBOLS

MAGEN DAVID

The Magen David (*Shield of David*) is a six-pointed star, usually known as the Star of David. It is used to decorate Synagogues and religious artefacts. It also features on the Israeli flag, which is often seen during Jewish festivals.

MENORAH

The Menorah is a seven-branched candelabrum. The original Menorah was made out of pure gold while the Israelites were being led through the desert by Moses. Later it was installed in the Temple in Jerusalem, where the seven lamps were kept continuously alight.

Sikhism

THERE IS ONE GOD,
Eternal Truth is God's name,
Creator of all things and the all-pervading spirit.
Fearless and without hatred,
Timeless and formless.
Beyond birth and death,
Self-enlightened.
By the grace of the Guru God is known.

The Mool Mantar

BACKGROUND INFORMATION

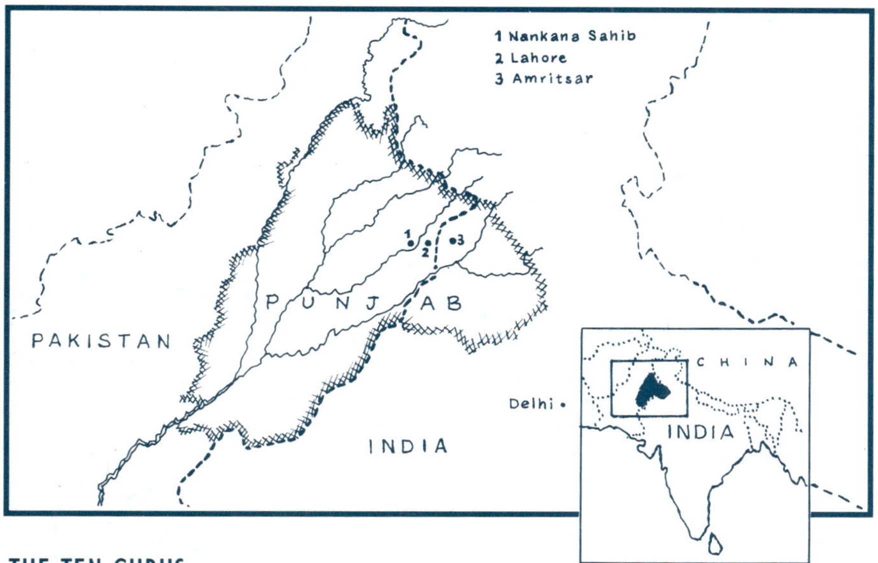

ORIGINS

Sikhism originated in the Punjab, which today lies partly in Pakistan and partly in north-west India. Punjab means 'five rivers', and it is a very fertile area.

The Sikh faith developed at the end of the fifteenth century, when the Punjab (comprising part of the Moghul Empire) was under Muslim rule. The early Sikh community faced terrible persecution and many Sikhs were martyred.

Sikhs believe that their religion was revealed to humankind through ten historical figures, each of whom is called a Guru. The last of the human Gurus was succeeded by the Guru Granth Sahib (the Sikh holy book). The ten human Gurus and the Guru Granth Sahib are greatly revered.

THE TEN GURUS

The ten human Gurus are said to have shared the same truth, to have possessed the same distinctive insight into God and even to have held the same basic identity. Sikhs say that they are like ten candles which have been lit one from another.

The ten Gurus are:

Guru Nanak	*(1469-1538 CE)*
Guru Angad	*(1504-1552 CE)*
Guru Amar Das	*(1479-1574 CE)*
Guru Ram Das	*(1534-1581 CE)*
Guru Arjan	*(1563-1606 CE)*
Guru Har Gobind	*(1595-1664 CE)*
Guru Har Rai	*(1630-1661 CE)*
Guru Krishan	*(1656-1664 CE)*
Guru Tegh Bahadur	*(1621-1675 CE)*
Guru Gobind Singh	*(1666-1708 CE)*

Below: *Guru Nanak surrounded by the other nine Sikh Gurus (with haloes) and his followers Bala and Mardana.*

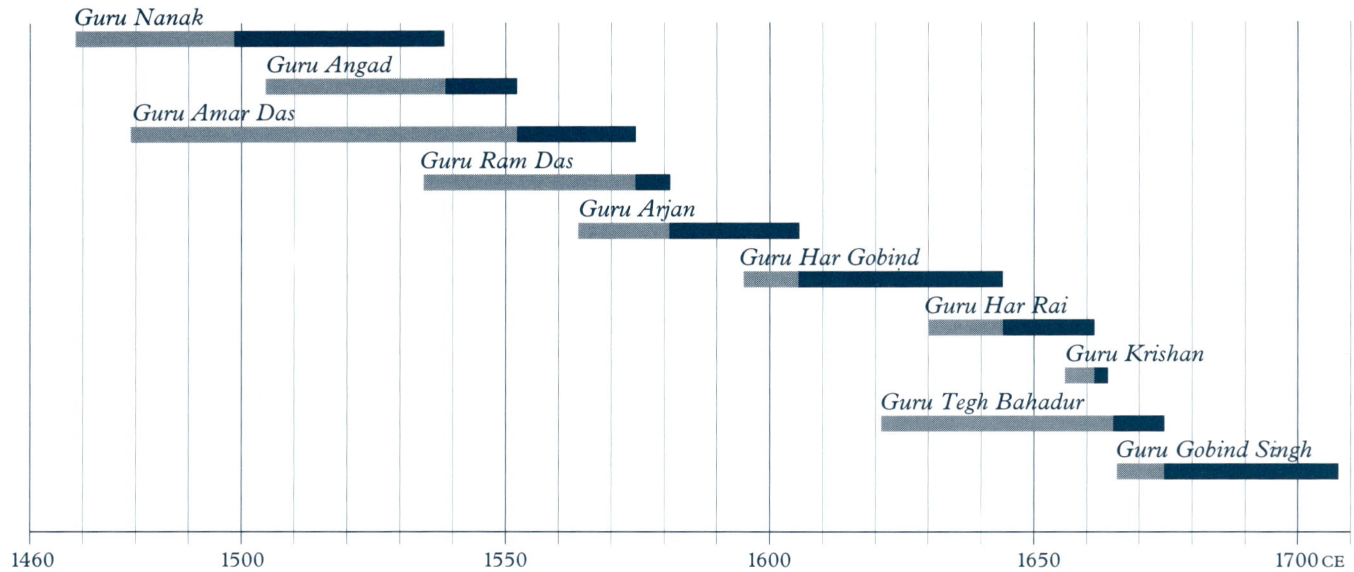

GURU NANAK

Guru Nanak (the founder of Sikhism) was born in Talwandi village, which is now in Pakistan. He came from a Hindu family and many of his neighbours were Muslims. Guru Nanak was taken away from school when he was still young because his father felt he was spending too much time thinking about God instead of studying. His father wanted him to work, and so he became a cowherd.

Above: *Guru Nanak visiting Makkah, the Muslim sacred city. He travelled widely trying to unite people in the belief that there is one God.*
Inset: *Guru Nanak.*

Many stories are told about the early stage of Guru Nanak's life. One day, in the heat of the sun, he fell asleep. A deadly cobra slid over him. One of his father's friends was horrified to see the cobra raise its head as if to strike at the sleeping boy. As he watched, however, he realised that the cobra was protecting Guru Nanak from the heat of the sun by casting a shadow over him. Even snakes treated Guru Nanak with reverence!

Guru Nanak married when he was 18 and became a storekeeper. About ten years later he went through a profound religious experience. Every day he observed the Hindu custom of ritual bathing. One morning he went as usual to the river to bathe, but this time he did not return. His family mourned their loss, but after three days he reappeared saying that he had been drinking nectar at God's court and proclaiming that there are 'neither Hindus nor Muslims, only brothers and sisters'. One of Guru Nanak's hymns describes the effect of his experience:

'I was a minstrel out of work,
The Lord gave me employment.
The mighty one instructed me,
"Night and day, sing my praise".'

For the next twenty years, Guru Nanak travelled thousands of miles on missionary journeys. In about 1521 CE he founded a village called Kartarpur, where he established the first Sikh community. His disciples came to be known as Sikhs. The word Sikh derives from a Punjabi verb which means 'to learn'.

At the age of 70, Guru Nanak realised that he was dying. He knew that he must choose a successor and so he thought of a test that would help him choose wisely. A heap of muddy grass was lying in a field and Guru Nanak asked his two sons to carry it home. They refused, telling him to ask one of his disciples to do it. A disciple called Lehna immediately ran forward and picked up the grass. As a further test, Guru Nanak threw a rupee into a pool of dirty water. Without hesitation, Lehna recovered it. Nanak chose Lehna to be his successor, naming him Angad (*My Limb*). That night Guru Nanak died.

GURU GOBIND SINGH

Guru Gobind Singh became the tenth Guru at a time when Sikhs were being persecuted by the Moghul Emperor of India. He realised that if Sikhism was to survive, members of the religion needed a strong sense of communal identity.

In 1699 CE, at the festival of Baisakhi (see page 96), Guru Gobind Singh called all the Sikhs together at Anandpur. He emerged from a tent carrying a drawn sword. He called out five times for volunteers who were prepared to die for their belief in God and in their Guru.

Five Sikhs eventually went forward and were taken into the tent one by one. Each time there was a swish of a sword and the Guru emerged alone, his sword now covered in blood. After the fifth Sikh had been taken into the tent, the Guru was followed out by all five Sikhs dressed in saffron coloured uniforms and carrying their own swords.

Guru Gobind Singh announced to the gathered Sikhs that the Panj Piare (*the Five Beloved Ones*) were now his brothers, the first of an army of soldier-saints called the Khalsa (*the Community of the Pure*). Their equality and unity was confirmed by the drinking of Amrit (*nectar*, a mixture of sugar and water) and the wearing of the Panj Kakke (*the Five Ks*–see page 100).

Twenty thousand Sikhs received Amrit that day and joined the Khalsa. All males were given the name Singh (*Lion*) and all females the name Kaur (*Princess*). Guru Gobind Singh told them they must always stand up to their enemies, protect the weak and help the poor.

Top: *Guru Gobind Singh.*
Above: *Guru Gobind Singh and his wife, Mata Sahib Kaur, preparing Amrit for the Panj Piare at the first initiation ceremony.*

Guru Gobind Singh died in 1708 CE. Before his death (from a stab wound), he declared that there would be no more human Gurus. Instead, his successor would be the Guru Granth Sahib, the holy book of Sikhism.

SIKHS TODAY

With a worldwide population of approximately 19 million, Sikhism is small in global terms. Over 80% of Sikhs live in the Punjab. The Sikh community in Britain (estimated to be around 400,000) is the largest outside the Indian sub-continent.

BELIEFS AND WAY OF LIFE

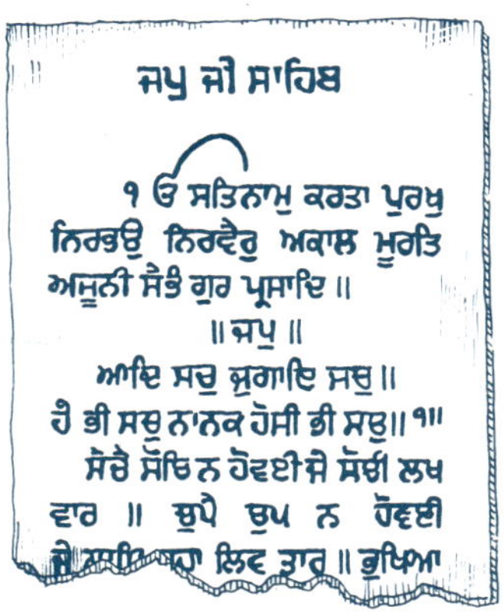

Top: *A brass ornament comprising the words 'Ik Onkar' (*'There is one God'*), the first words of the Mool Mantar, a reminder to Sikhs of Guru Nanak's desire to stop the distrust between people of different religions.*
Above: *The Mool Mantar, the first words of the Guru Granth Sahib.*

BASIC BELIEFS

The central ideas and beliefs of Sikhism relate closely in some respects to those of Islam and Hinduism, but it is important to appreciate that they derive from independent revelation. Like Muslims, Sikhs are strictly monotheistic, holding that there is only one God. Like Hindus, Sikhs believe that the goal of life is to be united with God. Both Sikhs and Hindus believe in reincarnation and in related ideas such as Karma (the law of cause and effect) and Mukti, the Sikh interpretation of Moksha (liberation from the cycle of life, death and rebirth).

GOD

The basic statement of Sikh belief is the Mool Mantar (*basic* or *essential teaching*), which describes the attributes of God in gender-free terms:

੧ੳ	*There is one God,*
ਸਤਿ ਨਾਮੁ	*Eternal Truth is God's name,*
ਕਰਤਾ ਪੁਰਖ	*Creator of all things and the all-pervading spirit.*
ਨਿਰ ਭਉ	*Fearless and without hatred,*
ਨਿਰ ਵੈਰੁ	*Timeless and formless.*
ਅਕਾਲ ਮੂਰਤਿ	*Beyond birth and death,*
ਅਜੂਨੀ ਸੈਭੰ	*Self-enlightened.*
ਗੁਰ ਪ੍ਰਸਾਦਿ ॥	*By the grace of the Guru God is known.*

Every section of the Guru Granth Sahib begins with the Mool Mantar, and it is recited daily as the first part of the Japji Sahib, the morning prayer which comprises the first chapter of the Guru Granth Sahib.

God is known to Sikhs by many names. Nam Simran (meditation on the attributes of God) is an important religious activity for Sikhs. This can involve the recitation of passages of scripture or the repetition of one or other of the two names of God traditionally used in worship: 'Satnam' (*True Name*) and 'Waheguru' (*Wonderful Lord*). Waheguru, which is an exclamation of praise, is the term for God most frequently used by Sikhs.

THE PURPOSE OF LIFE

For Sikhs, the purpose of life is to achieve the reunion of the human soul with God. Reunion with God and release from the cycle of reincarnation are achieved by living in accordance with the teaching of the Gurus. This involves Sewa (*service* to all human beings) and acceptance of Hukam (*God's will*).

DIET

Sikhs are encouraged to avoid alcohol and tobacco. Halal meat (meat from animals killed according to Muslim law) is forbidden. Many Sikhs are vegetarians.

WRITINGS

THE GURU GRANTH SAHIB

The Guru Granth Sahib is the Sikh holy book and it is always treated with immense respect. It was compiled by Guru Arjan, the fifth Guru. It contains writings by Guru Nanak, other Gurus, prominent Sikhs and some non-Sikhs.

The Guru Granth Sahib contains no narrative. It consists entirely of Shabads (hymns) and poems designed to be sung. The words of the Guru Granth Sahib are full of passionate praise for God and are intended to be inspirational. All copies of the Guru Granth Sahib are identical, with 1,430 pages written in Gurmukhi, the script in which the Punjabi language is written.

Before Guru Gobind Singh died, he stated that the Guru Granth Sahib was to be his successor. Sikhs regard the book as the final and everlasting Guru: the voice of the ten human Gurus. The book is treated with great reverence and whenever it is moved, it is carried on a person's head.

The Guru Granth Sahib is the focus of attention in the prayer hall. It is placed on the Manji, a dais which rests on a platform called the Takht (*throne*). Above the holy book is the Chanani, a piece of cloth attached to the four poles of a wooden canopy called the Palki.

During worship the Guru Granth Sahib is read by a trained reader called a Granthi, and an attendant waves a Chauri over it (see page 102). A Chauri is a fan traditionally made of yak hairs. It is a symbol of the authority of the scriptures. The Guru Granth Sahib is kept covered by cloths called Rumala (see page 102), except when being read, and it is never touched with unwashed hands. When it is carried in, everyone stands and bows towards it. It is thought to be disrespectful to turn one's back on this most holy of books, and when sitting before it, care is taken to ensure that the soles of the feet do not face it.

Above: *A Chauri is waved over the Guru Granth Sahib.*

The Guru Granth Sahib helps to determine a Sikh's name (see page 97), and Sikhs are initiated and married in its presence (see pages 97 and 98). On special occasions, the Guru Granth Sahib is read continuously from beginning to end. This reading, which takes about 48 hours, is called an Akhand Path.

Some Sikhs keep a copy of the Guru Granth Sahib in the home, where it is kept in a room set aside solely for that purpose. Many Sikhs also possess a small book called a Nit Nem, which contains extracts from the Guru Granth Sahib and other sacred writings, such as the Dasam Granth (*see below*). The Nit Nem is used for daily prayers.

THE DASAM GRANTH

The Dasam Granth contains Shabads (*hymns*) and poems written by Guru Gobind Singh, some of which are used in Sikh ceremonies.

FESTIVALS

Sikh festivals fall into two categories: Melas (fairs) and Gurpurbs. Divali and Hola Mohalla are Melas. The Gurpurbs comprise Baisakhi and anniversaries of the birth or death of one of the ten Gurus.

***Above:** The Nishan Sahib, the yellow, triangular flag with the Sikh symbol that flies outside every Gurdwara.*

BAISAKHI (13 April)

The Sikh new year begins with Baisakhi, an ancient festival which in the Punjab traditionally marks the start of the corn harvest. It was at Baisakhi in 1699 CE that the Khalsa (*the Community of the Pure*) was founded by Guru Gobind Singh (see page 93), and today the celebrations recall this event.

An Akhand Path (continuous reading of the Guru Granth Sahib) leads up to Baisakhi. On the day itself, Sikhs bathe or shower and put on new clothes. They go to the Gurdwara where the flagpole is unwrapped and cleaned with yoghurt and water. The cloth around the flagpole and the Nishan Sahib (the Sikh flag–see page 102) are ceremoniously renewed.

DIVALI (October/November)

Divali is celebrated throughout the Indian sub-continent by both Hindus and Sikhs, but while Hindus recall the story of Rama and Sita, Sikhs remember how Guru Har Gobind rescued 52 Hindu princes (see story below).

Divali is an autumn festival, during which Gurdwaras and homes are lit with lamps and there are bonfires and firework displays. Children are given sweetmeats and gifts are exchanged.

The story behind Divali

The sixth Sikh Guru, Guru Har Gobind, failed to pay a fine that had been imposed on his father, Guru Arjan. As a result, he was imprisoned by the Moghul emperor, Jehangir. When Jehangir personally investigated the case, he rejected the charges and ordered the Guru's release.

Imprisoned with the Guru were 52 Hindu princes, all of them innocent. The Guru refused to leave the prison unless they were released too. Jehangir told Guru Har Gobind that as many of them could go free as could hold on to the Guru's coat as he walked along the narrow passage that led out of the prison.

In order to rescue the princes, Guru Har Gobind had a special coat made with long tassels. All 52 princes were able to hold on to the tassels as the Guru walked with them to freedom.

HOLA MOHALLA (February/March)

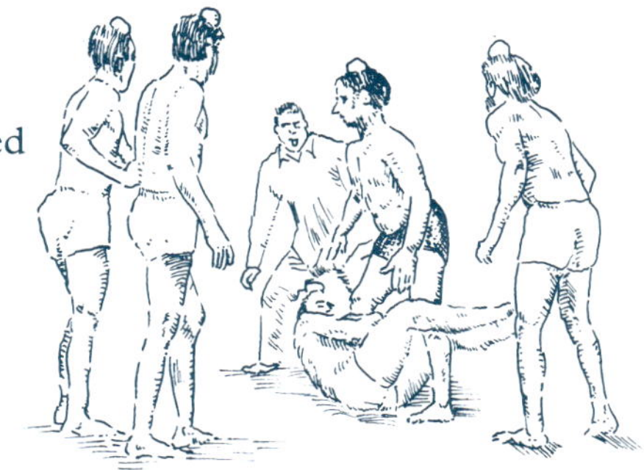

Hola Mohalla takes place at the same time as the Hindu spring festival of Holi. In order to divert the attention of Sikhs from what he considered to be the rather trivial festivities associated with Holi, Guru Gobind Singh summoned the Sikhs to Anandpur to take part in mock battles. Today, Hola Mohalla (*attack and place of attack*) is seriously observed only in Anandpur, where there are trials of combat such as wrestling matches, archery competitions and fencing tournaments. The festival opens with a fair and ends with a carnival procession.

GURPURBS

The most important Gurpurbs are the birthdays of Guru Nanak and Guru Gobind Singh and the martyrdoms of Guru Arjan and Guru Tegh Bahadur. During every Gurpurb, there is an Akhand Path (a continuous reading of the Guru Granth Sahib). In India and the Punjab, the Guru Granth Sahib is carried in procession through the streets escorted by five men representing the Panj Piare (*the Five Beloved Ones*—see page 93).

RITES OF PASSAGE

BIRTH

Top: *Team game, kabadi, played during Hola Mohalla.*
Above: *The martyrdom of Guru Arjan.*
Below: *The naming ceremony.*

Birth and Naming

As soon as a new-born baby has been washed, the words of the Mool Mantar (see page 94) are sometimes whispered into the child's ear. Then a drop of honey may be placed on the baby's tongue as a symbol of the sweetness of the Guru's words.

Some weeks later, the baby will be taken to the Gurdwara so that the family can give thanks and so that the child can be named. Some families organise an Akhand Path (continuous reading of the Guru Granth Sahib), and a few drops of Amrit (a mixture of sugar and water) may be placed on the baby's lips with a Khanda (double-sided sword).

For the naming of the child, the Guru Granth Sahib is opened at random by the Granthi (the reader of the Guru Granth Sahib and the leader of the service). The first letter of the first word on the left-hand page will be the first letter of the baby's name. The parents quickly decide upon the name, which is then announced. The surname will always be Singh (*Lion*) for boys, and Kaur (*Princess*) for girls (see page 93).

COMING OF AGE

The Amrit Ceremony

Both male and female Sikhs are initiated into the Khalsa (*the Community of the Pure*) from about the age of 16. Before people can join the Khalsa, they must show that they are living according to the Sikh way of life.

The Amrit ceremony is a private event which usually takes place in the Gurdwara. It is essentially a recreation of the occasion when Guru Gobind Singh founded the Khalsa (see page 93). The ceremony is conducted by five respected members of the Khalsa, who are dressed to look like the Panj Piare (*the Five Beloved Ones*). The initiates are reminded of the duties of a Sikh:

To accept the teachings of the Guru Granth Sahib.
To wear the Panj Kakke (the Five Ks–see page 101).
Not to smoke or take drugs.
To accept other Sikhs as equals.
To give a tenth of one's income to charity.
To be prepared to sacrifice all for the Sikh faith.

Amrit (*nectar*, a mixture of sugar and water) is stirred with the Khanda (double-sided sword) in a steel bowl. It is given to the initiates to drink and then it is sprinkled on to their eyes and hair.

The Mool Mantar is chanted, Ardas (*prayer*) is said and Karah Parshad (*sanctified food*–see page 100) is eaten.

Top: *The Amrit ceremony.*
Above: *A Sikh bridegroom and his bride.*

MARRIAGE

Sikhs are usually expected to marry within the religion and in most cases marriages are arranged between the families involved. Guru Nanak taught that within marriage, men and women are equal. Divorce and re-marriage are permitted, but they are rare.

The marriage ceremony takes place during morning worship at the Gurdwara. The groom and his male companions arrive first. The groom, wearing a muslin scarf and a red or pink turban, sits in front of the Guru Granth Sahib awaiting the arrival of the bride. She joins him, dressed completely in red and gold. She wears a sari or shalwar and kameez (trousers and tunic), with a dupatta (headscarf) over her head. She is adorned with many pieces of gold jewellery, and her hands and feet are decorated with Mendhi patterns made from henna.

The Granthi, who leads the service, reads from the Guru Granth Sahib and explains the meaning of Sikh marriage. The couple bow to the Guru Granth Sahib, and put on garlands which the bride's father has brought. He then ties his daughter's dupatta to the groom's muslin scarf. As the Lavan (a marriage hymn composed by Guru Ram Das for his daughter's wedding) is sung, the groom leads the bride four times in a clockwise direction around the Guru Granth Sahib.

The service ends with the distribution of Karah Parshad (sanctified food).

DEATH

Beliefs

Sikhs believe that one is born into the Sikh religion as a result of good Karma (*action*): as a reward for living a good previous life. As a Sikh, one can hear the true word of God and by one's actions one can achieve Mukti (*liberation* from the cycle of life, death and rebirth). To die as a Sikh is to achieve possible union with God. For this reason Sikhs do not openly mourn for the dead.

Customs

After death the body is washed, clothed and dressed with the Panj Kakke (*the Five Ks*–see page 100). In India and the Punjab, the body is cremated in the open air on a funeral pyre. In the West, the cremation takes place in a crematorium. At the cremation, the Sohila (the evening hymn) is sung and Ardas (*prayer*) is said.

After the cremation, there is a service in the Gurdwara, which ends with the sharing of Karah Parshad (sanctified food). The family of the deceased make arrangements for a complete reading of the Guru Granth Sahib to take place. This may be an Akhand Path (continuous reading) or a Saptah (seven-day reading) or a Dassehra (ten-day reading).

The dead person's ashes are scattered with flowers on to a river. Sikh teaching discourages the erection of tombs or monuments.

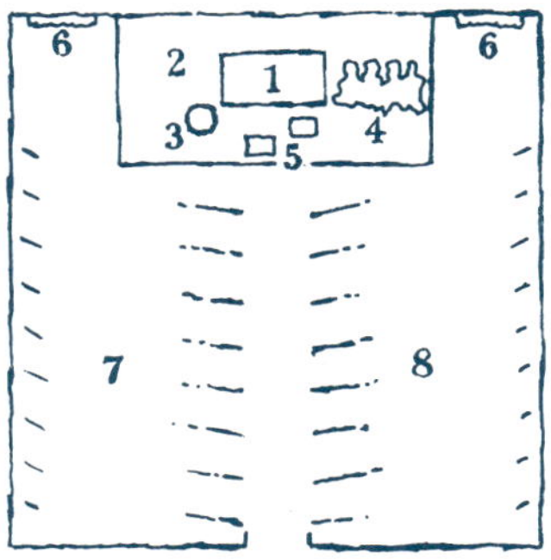

Above: *Plan of a typical Gurdwara;*
1 Guru Granth Sahib on its Manji (dais) under the Palki (canopy)
2 Takht (platform)
3 Bowl containing Karah Parshad
4 Ragis (musicians)
5 Offerings or gifts of money or milk and fruit
6 Pictures of Gurus
7 Women seated on the floor
8 Men seated on the floor.

PLACES OF WORSHIP

THE GURDWARA

The Gurdwara (*the doorway to the Guru*) is primarily a place for worship, but it is also a meeting place and a community centre. In addition to the hall used for worship, there is always a Langar (*Guru's kitchen*), a communal kitchen and dining-hall. There may also be a library, classrooms, offices and rooms where visitors can sleep. From a flagpole outside the Gurdwara flies the Nishan Sahib, a saffron-coloured triangular flag bearing the Khanda, the symbol of the Sikh religion (see page 102).

The worship hall is carpeted and sparsely furnished. There are sometimes pictures around the walls depicting Guru Nanak, Guru Gobind Singh and the Harmandir (*the Golden Temple*–see page 100). The room is colourfully decorated with streamers, lights and tinsel. Dominating the hall is the Palki, the canopy under which the Guru Granth Sahib is placed (see page 95).

Below: *The Granthi reads from the Guru Granth Sahib.*

WORSHIP AT THE GURDWARA

Sikh worship tends to be informal. During the service, which may last several hours, worshippers enter and leave when they want. Before going into the worship hall, hands are washed, heads are covered and shoes are removed. Upon entering the worship hall, each person bows right down before the Guru Granth Sahib. Offerings of money are placed in a box placed in front of the Takht (the platform on which the Guru Granth Sahib rests–see page 95). The congregation sits on the floor, women on one side and men on the other. It is considered disrespectful to turn one's back on the Guru Granth Sahib or to sit with the soles of the feet facing towards it.

There are no priests in Sikhism. Any member of the congregation (man or woman) may read from the Guru Granth Sahib, although this is usually done by a specially trained Granthi. In addition to the readings, Shabads (*hymns*) from the Guru Granth Sahib are sung. The musicians, usually including a harmonium player and a tabla player, sit to one side of the Takht.

At the end of the service, everyone stands for a formal prayer called Ardas. While Ardas is being said, a mixture of flour or semolina, butter, sugar and water is sometimes stirred with a Kirpan (a short sword). This sanctified food is called Karah Parshad. After Ardas, each person is given a small amount of Karah Parshad to eat with the right hand. When the service has ended, it is usual for everyone to stay on in order to share a full meal in the Langar (kitchen or dining-hall).

THE HARMANDIR AT AMRITSAR

Above: *The Harmandir at Amritsar, the holiest place in the Sikh religion.*

The fourth Guru, Guru Ram Das, founded the city of Amritsar in the Punjab and had a large pool constructed there. Amritsar means Pool of Nectar. His successor, Guru Arjan, organised the building of a temple covered in gold that stands in the pool. The Harmandir (*the Golden Temple*) is the most important holy place and pilgrimage centre for Sikhs. The pool is used for ritual bathing. The Harmandir has four entrances to show that all who wish to enter may do so. From each entrance people walk down steps into the worship hall as a sign of humility.

RITUAL OBJECTS AND ARTEFACTS

CLOTHING

Panj Kakke
It is a religious duty for Sikh men and women to wear the Panj Kakke (*the Five Ks*) as symbols of their faith. The Five Ks all begin with the letter K in Punjabi:

Kesh: uncut hair (a symbol of holiness)
Kangha: comb used to keep hair in place (a symbol of orderliness)
Kara: circular steel bangle (a symbol of strength, unity and the eternal nature of God)
Kirpan: sword (a symbol of the desire to defend the weak) – many Sikhs wear a small Kirpan on a sling under their outer clothing and in Britain many wear a miniature replica or a Kirpan badge
Kachera: shorts worn as underwear (a reminder of the Sikhs' fighting past, they were originally worn to give warriors greater freedom of movement in battle)

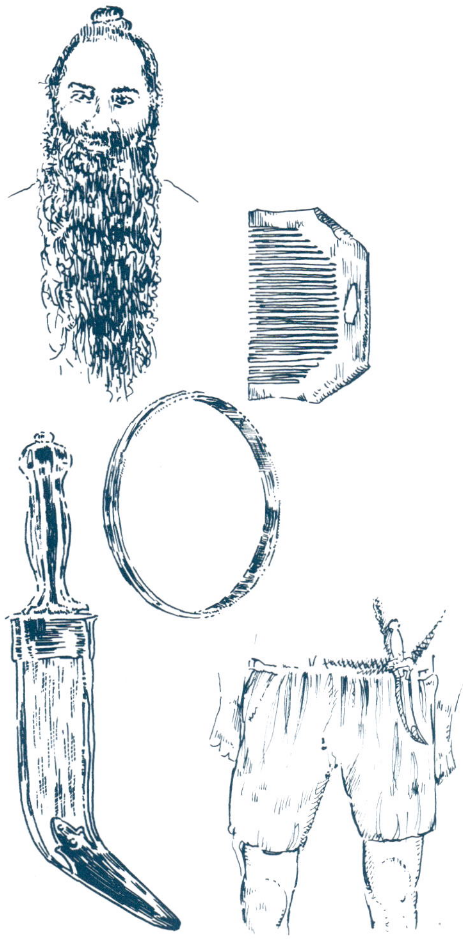

Turban
In order to keep their uncut hair tidy, Sikh men wear turbans.

Turbans are pieces of cloth about five metres long and a metre wide. Before the turban is wrapped around the head, the hair is twisted into a knot on top of the head and kept in place with the Kangha (comb – see above).

Boys start wearing turbans when their hair is long enough, usually when they are about eleven years old. A boy's first turban is tied by a respected member of the Sikh community in the presence of the Guru Granth Sahib.

Above: *The five Ks.*
Left: *Tying a turban.*

Boys who are too young to wear turbans tie their hair in a top-knot. This is then covered with a Patka (a square piece of cloth about the size of a handkerchief).

Shalwar, Kameez and Dupatta

The shalwar, kameez and dupatta are traditionally worn by Sikh women:

Shalwar: long, loose trousers.
Kameez: long, loose tunic.
Dupatta: long scarf worn over the head and shoulders.

Garlands

Bright and colourful garlands are worn on special occasions such as weddings and festivals.

IMAGES OF THE GURUS AND THE HARMANDIR

Sikh homes are often decorated with framed pictures or wall-hangings depicting the Gurus, particularly Guru Nanak and Guru Gobind Singh, and the Harmandir (*the Golden Temple*–see page 100). Guru Nanak, with a long white beard, is shown sitting cross-legged with his right hand raised as though he is greeting or blessing the viewer. Guru Gobind Singh is shown richly dressed in full warrior's regalia, with a bow over his shoulder and a quiver full of arrows on his back.

KHANDA AND STEEL BOWL

The Khanda is a double-edged sword used to stir Patases (sugar bubbles or crystals) and water together to make Amrit. The Amrit is mixed in a steel bowl, from which everyone drinks during the Amrit ceremony (see page 97).

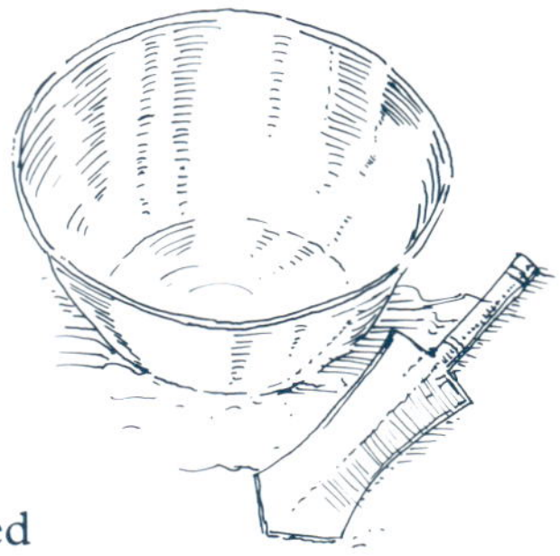

GURU GRANTH SAHIB

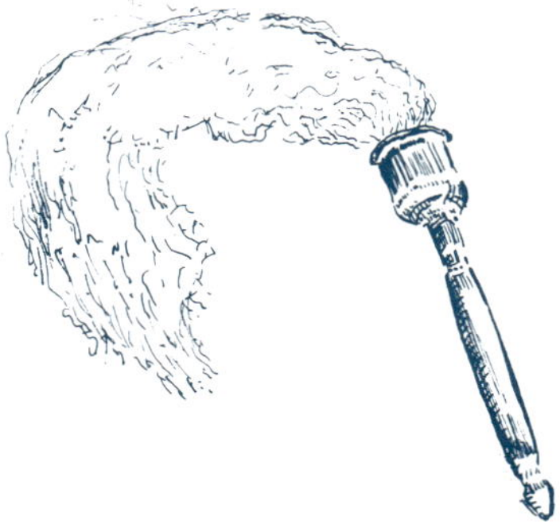

Rumala (see page 95)

The Guru Granth Sahib is covered in ornate cloths called Rumala.

Chauri (see page 95)

The Chauri is a fan traditionally made of yak hairs with an ornate silver handle. It is a symbol of the authority of the Guru Granth Sahib, and it is waved over the scriptures as a mark of respect. It is inappropriate to refer to the Chauri as a fly whisk.

PRAYER

Nit Nem

The Nit Nem is a small book containing extracts from the Guru Granth Sahib and other sacred writings, such as the Dasam Granth (see page 95). The Nit Nem is used for daily prayers.

SYMBOLS

KHANDA

The Khanda, the Sikh emblem, is used widely by Sikhs. It appears inside the Gurdwara and outside on the Nishan Sahib (Sikh flag). It is used as an ornament in the home, and many Sikhs wear Khanda badges.

The design of the Khanda incorporates three Sikh artefacts. In the centre is the double-edged sword (also called a Khanda) used to stir Amrit. Around the double-edged sword is the Kara (*steel bangle*). On either side of the Kara are two Kirpans (*swords*).

HARRISON COUNTY PRIMARY SCHOOL
HARRISON ROAD
FAREHAM
HAMPSHIRE PO16 7EQ